How to Ask
Survey Questions

2nd edition

THE SURVEY KIT, Second Edition

Purposes: The purposes of this 10-volume Kit are to enable readers to prepare and conduct surveys and to help readers become better users of survey results. Surveys are conducted to collect information; surveyors ask questions of people on the telephone, face-to-face, and by mail. The questions can be about attitudes, beliefs, and behavior as well as socioeconomic and health status. To do a good survey, one must know how to plan and budget for all survey tasks, how to ask questions, how to design the survey (research) project, how to sample respondents, how to collect reliable and valid information, and how to analyze and report the results.

Users: The Kit is for students in undergraduate and graduate classes in the social and health sciences and for individuals in the public and private sectors who are responsible for conducting and using surveys. Its primary goal is to enable users to prepare surveys and collect data that are accurate and useful for primarily practical purposes. Sometimes, these practical purposes overlap with the objectives of scientific research, and so survey researchers will also find the Kit useful.

Format of the Kit: All books in the series contain instructional objectives, exercises and answers, examples of surveys in use and illustrations of survey questions, guidelines for action, checklists of dos and don'ts, and annotated references.

Volumes in The Survey Kit:

1. **The Survey Handbook, 2nd**
   Arlene Fink
2. **How to Ask Survey Questions, 2nd**
   Arlene Fink
3. **How to Conduct Self-Administered and Mail Surveys, 2nd**
   Linda B. Bourque and Eve P. Fielder
4. **How to Conduct Telephone Surveys, 2nd**
   Linda B. Bourque and Eve P. Fielder
5. **How to Conduct In-Person Interviews for Surveys, 2nd**
   Sabine Mertens Oishi
6. **How to Design Survey Studies, 2nd**
   Arlene Fink
7. **How to Sample in Surveys, 2nd**
   Arlene Fink
8. **How to Assess and Interpret Survey Psychometrics, 2nd**
   Mark S. Litwin
9. **How to Manage, Analyze, and Interpret Survey Data, 2nd**
   Arlene Fink
10. **How to Report on Surveys, 2nd**
    Arlene Fink

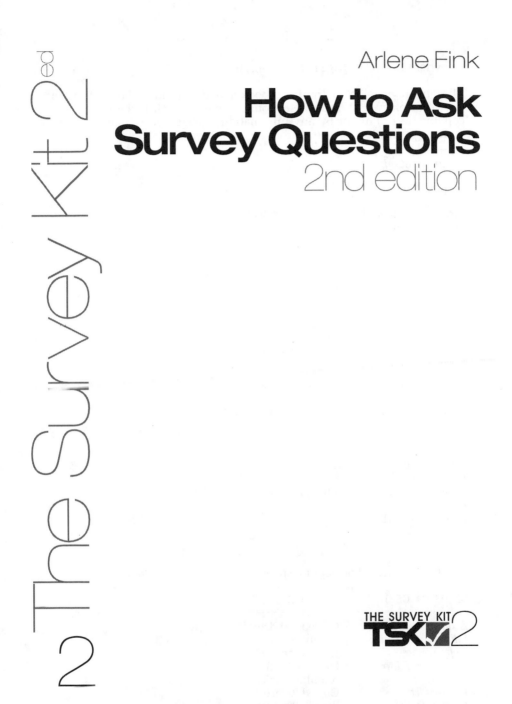

Arlene Fink

How to Ask
Survey Questions

2nd edition

The Survey Kit 2ed

2 The Survey Kit 2

THE SURVEY KIT
TSK 2

SAGE Publications
International Educational and Professional Publisher
Thousand Oaks ▪ London ▪ New Delhi

For information:

Sage Publications, Inc.
2455 Teller Road
Thousand Oaks, California 91320
E-mail: order@sagepub.com

Sage Publications Ltd.
6 Bonhill Street
London EC2A 4PU
United Kingdom

Sage Publications India Pvt. Ltd.
M-32 Market
Greater Kailash I
New Delhi 110 048 India

Printed in the United States of America

Library of Congress Cataloging-in-Publication Data

The survey kit.—2nd ed.
        p. cm.
Includes bibliographical references.
ISBN 0-7619-2510-4 (set : pbk.)
1. Social surveys. 2. Health surveys. I. Fink, Arlene.
HN29 .S724 2002
300'.723—dc21   2002012405

This book is printed on acid-free paper.

02 03 04 05 10 9 8 7 6 5 4 3 2 1

Acquisitions Editor:	C. Deborah Laughton
Editorial Assistant:	Veronica Novak
Copy Editor:	Judy Selhorst
Production Editor:	Diane S. Foster
Typesetter:	Bramble Books
Proofreader:	Cheryl Rivard
Cover Designer:	Ravi Balasuriya
Production Designer:	Michelle Lee

Contents

How to Ask Survey Questions:
Learning Objectives

The aim of this book is to guide you in preparing and using reliable and valid survey questions. The specific objectives are as follows:

- Understand a survey's cultural, psychological, economic, and political context by doing the following:

  - Identifying specific purposes

  - Preparing appropriately worded, meaningful questions for participants

  - Clarifying research and other objectives

  - Determining a feasible number of questions

  - Standardizing the questioner

  - Standardizing the response choices

- Ask valid questions that
  - Make sense to the respondent

  - Are concrete

  - Use time periods that are related to the importance of the question

  - Use conventional language

  - Are appropriate in length

- Use loaded words cautiously

- Avoid biasing words

- Avoid two-edgers

- Avoid negative phrasing

- Are appropriate in light of the characteristics and uses of closed and open questions

- Distinguish among response formats that use nominal, ordinal, and numerical measurement

- Are correctly prepared

■ Correctly ask questions by doing the following:

- Using response categories that are meaningfully grouped

- Choosing appropriate types of response options

- Balancing all responses on scales

- Selecting neutral categories appropriately

- Determining how many points to include on rating scales

- Choosing appropriate placement for the positive and negative ends of scales

- Determining the proper use of skip patterns

- Apply special questioning techniques to survey behaviors, knowledge, attitudes, and demographics
- Describe the characteristics of focus group questions
- Identify the characteristics and uses of factorial questions
- Identify the characteristics and uses of conjoint analysis questions
- Understand the principles underlying questions in Internet surveys

1

Asking Questions: A Matter of Context

A survey is a system for collecting information from or about people to describe, compare, or explain their knowledge, attitudes, and behavior. Surveys are taken to gather information about people's political and consumer choices, to find out about how people use health services, to determine the numbers of people in the labor force, and to gather opinions on just about everything, from aardvarks to zyzzyvas. Individuals, communities, schools, businesses, and researchers use surveys to find out about people by asking questions about feelings, motivations, plans, beliefs, and personal backgrounds. Survey questions are typically arranged into mailed or self-administered questionnaires or into instruments used by interviewers in conducting in-person (face-to-face) or telephone interviews. Because questions are the focus of many surveys, it is essential that you learn how to ask them, in both written and spoken form.

The ways in which survey questions are asked can prescribe the answers, as Example 1.1 illustrates. As you can see, surveyors with competing agendas can come up with entirely different questions, responses, and interpretations regarding the same survey topic.

EXAMPLE 1.1
The Relationships Among
Questions, People, and Information

Three survey experts were invited to present the results of their survey "American Views on Taxation." Expert A's presentation was titled "Most Americans Support Increased Taxes for Worthy Purposes." Expert B's speech was called "Some Americans Support Increased Taxes for Worthy Purposes." Expert C's talk was named "Few Americans Support Increased Taxes for Worthy Purposes." A review of the experts' talks and original surveys revealed three questions:

Expert A's: Would you support increased taxes to pay for education programs for very poor children?

Expert B's: Would you support an increase in your taxes to pay for education programs for very poor children?

Expert C's: Would you support a 10% increase in your taxes to pay for education programs for very poor children?

Surveys are used to gather information for use in research and evaluation studies and in planning programs and setting policy in health, education, business, and government. This book focuses on guidelines that will help you to ask questions appropriately for all these survey uses.

The selection and wording of questions are strongly influenced by the survey's context: its purposes, who asks the questions, how they are asked, who answers them, and the characteristics of respondents and responses. Consider the two surveys described in Example 1.2, which are different in several ways. Such differences influence surveyors' choices of questions as well as the characteristics and number of questions, as shown in Example 1.3.

EXAMPLE 1.2
Survey Questions and Their Contexts

Survey 1

Lancaster, a community of about 150,000 people, is planning programs to prevent child abuse and family violence. The community intends to conduct a survey in which families are asked to identify their problems and suggest solutions to them. The results will be used to guide the development of programs to prevent and treat alcohol abuse, social isolation, and unemployment. These problems and others like them are known to be prevalent in the community. Research has linked them to abuse and violence.

Parents with school-age children in 4 of the city's 10 school districts will be mailed a survey questionnaire to complete in the privacy of their homes. The questionnaire, which focuses on educational needs, takes 20 minutes to complete and will be provided to respondents in all five of the languages most commonly spoken in the community. All responses will be anonymous. The questionnaire will give respondents a list of statements and ask them to state, by placing a rating on a scale from 1 to 4, whether they strongly agree, agree, disagree, or strongly disagree with each. Prominent members of the community and the city have endorsed the questionnaire.

Example 1.2 continued

Survey 2

The Children's Clinic is a school-based clinic in a very-low-income area of a large city. The clinic intends to conduct a survey in which families and teachers will be asked to identify children's health problems (including medical and psychosocial issues) that the clinic might address. A sample of parents, teachers, health professionals, and children will be interviewed in person. Each interview will take 30 minutes. Interviews will be conducted in English or Spanish, depending on the first language of the respondent. About half the questions will ask respondents to give ratings and make rankings; the remainder will allow respondents to give answers in their own words. All responses will be confidential. A report of the results will be available in 12 months.

The two surveys described in Examples 1.2 and 1.3 aim to guide the development of programs and the focus of services to prevent child abuse and family violence and to promote health. Survey 1 is for parents only; Survey 2 is for parents, teachers, health professionals, and children. Because Survey 1 is self-administered, the surveyors must be certain that the questions can be understood by respondents without assistance from the survey team. The results of Survey 2 will require the surveyors to have special expertise in interpretation and classification of the responses that are given in the participants' own words. Survey 1's team will need resources for printing and mailing; the Survey 2 researchers will need funding for hiring and training interviewers. Because all answers on Survey 1 are anonymous, the surveyors may be able to ask questions about topics that named respondents might be reluctant to discuss. Although answers on Survey 2

EXAMPLE 1.3
Two Surveys

	Survey 1: A Mailed Questionnaire Concerning Child Abuse	Survey 2: Interviews About the Services of a School-Based Clinic	Effect on Questions
Purpose	Identify needs and solutions to guide program development	Identify needs to guide focus of clinic services	Survey 1: Questions are about education Survey 2: Questions are about health
Respondents	Parents of school-age children	Parents, teachers, health professionals, and children	Survey 1: Questions posed are for parents only Survey 2: Questions posed are for people of differing roles and ages
Surveyor	Self-administered, mailed questionnaire contains the questions	Interviewers ask questions face-to-face	Survey 1: Questions must be easily read and understood without outside assistance Survey 2: Questions must be worded so that they can be understood orally

Example 1.3 continued

	Survey 1: A Mailed Questionnaire Concerning Child Abuse	Survey 2: Interviews About the Services of a School-Based Clinic	Effect on Questions
Responses	Closed: Ratings made on a scale from 1 to 4	Some questions use ratings and rankings, the remainder rely on the respondent's own words	Survey 1: Responses can be translated on a scale from 1 to 4 Survey 2: Half the responses will come from ratings and rankings, the remainder will be in participants' own words
Timing	Survey takes 20 minutes	Survey takes 30 minutes	Survey 1: Respondents may not return questionnaires, or they may not answer all questions Survey 2: Time must be allocated for reading and interpreting respondents' answers
Resources	Need translation into five languages Survey must be printed and mailed	Need translation into English and Spanish Interviewers must be hired and trained	Survey 1: Expertise is needed in five languages Survey 2: Expertise is needed in two languages

Example 1.3 continued

	Survey 1: **A Mailed** **Questionnaire** **Concerning** **Child Abuse**	**Survey 2:** **Interviews About** **the Services of a** **School-Based** **Clinic**	**Effect on** **Questions**
Privacy	All responses will be anonymous	All responses will be confidential (codes will replace names)	Survey 1: "Sensitive" questions (e.g., about drug use and sexual habits) are more likely to be answered Survey 2: Must be a little more "careful" with sensitive questions, as respondents can be traced

will be kept confidential, the respondents will not have complete anonymity, and this may reduce their willingness to be frank in their answers. Survey 1 needs to be translated into five languages; Survey 2 is to be given only in English and Spanish.

You must understand fully your survey's purpose, the needs of the survey team, and the nature of your respondents (along with other considerations) before you begin to write your survey questions. The following checklist will help you to identify and understand your survey's context.

Checklist for Deciding the Survey's Context

✓ Identify the survey's specific purpose.

The purpose of a survey is its hoped-for outcome. Usually, you have a general purpose in mind—say, to find out about job satisfaction, preferences for certain products, or voting plans. If you are concerned with job satisfaction, for example, your survey should focus on that topic. Questions about respondents' previous jobs, hobbies, personal backgrounds, and so on, may not be relevant.

✓ Clarify the terms used to state the survey's purpose.

In Example 1.2, Survey 1's questions focus on educational needs, but the term *educational needs* is very general. Educational needs may include completing high school and obtaining vocational training as well as acquiring specific skills, such as how to be a parent, to cook, and to manage money.

Survey 2 in Example 1.2 is about the health needs of children. Definitions of health are far from uniform and vary according to culture. To select appropriate and usable definitions for your survey, you can review what is known and published about the topic you are addressing. You can also define terms yourself, but this may be problematic in that others may not be convinced of your definitions' validity. Sometimes, it is best to adopt already respected definitions and even, if possible, an already tested set of questions.

Your choices regarding the focus of your survey and the definitions used in survey questions sometimes become clear when you know your survey's specific objectives.

✓ **Be sure to have the specific objectives of the survey in place.**

The specific objectives of your survey are the precise goals you aim to meet with the information you collect. Sometimes, specific objectives are expressed as research hypotheses or questions; at other times, they take the form of statements. Consider these sample objectives for Survey 1 in Example 1.2:

1. Identify the most common needs for educational services

2. Determine the extent to which differences exist among the needs of parents of differing ethnicities/races

3. Determine the extent to which differences exist in needs between men and women

4. Identify whether parents are willing to participate in job retraining programs

5. Find out whether parents are satisfied with their current educational status

A specific set of objectives like these suggests a survey that asks questions about the following:

- Educational needs (Objective 1)

- Ethnicity/race (Objective 2)

- Gender (Objective 3)

- Willingness of respondents to participate in job retraining (Objective 4)

- Satisfaction of respondents with current educational status (Objective 5)

Suppose another surveyor added these objectives:

6. Compare younger and older parents in their needs to learn how to manage a household and care for a child

7. Determine the relationship between parents' education and method of disciplining children for mild, moderate, and severe infractions

To collect information to meet the new objectives, Survey 1 would need to add questions on the following:

- Age of parents

- How parents manage their household

- How parents care for their children

- Level of parents' education

- Methods for disciplining children for mild, moderate, and severe infractions

Before you can prepare a survey, you need to clarify or define all potentially imprecise or ambiguous terms that are likely to be used in the survey's specific questions. For the questions above, the imprecise terms are *needs, educational services, ethnicity/race, willingness, satisfaction, younger and older, effective household management, effective child care, discipline,* and *mild, moderate, and severe infractions*. Why are these terms ambiguous? No standard definition exists for any of them. What are needs, for example, and, of the very long list that you might create, which will be included on the survey? What is effective child care? What is discipline? How do you distinguish satisfied from dissatisfied parents?

EXERCISE

The following are four specific objectives for Survey 2 in Example 1.2:

1. Find out where children usually receive their health care

2. Identify barriers to using preventive health services, such as vaccinations

3. Identify whether differences exist in the health care needs of younger and older children of differing ethnicities/races

4. Compare the health statuses of boys and girls of differing ethnicities/races

For this exercise:

a. Add at least three more objectives

b. Describe the data that the survey must collect to meet all seven objectives (the first four above and the three you have added)

c. List all terms that will need to be defined or clarified before good questions can be written

● ●
SUGGESTED ANSWERS

Two additional objectives:

> 5. Compare the barriers to use of health services among older and younger parents whose children will use the clinic

> 6. Determine if respondents are satisfied with the quality of the health services their children currently receive

Data to be collected:

- Barriers to the use of health services
- Age
- Ethnicity/race
- Health status
- Satisfaction with quality of health services

Definitions and clarifications needed:

- Health services
- Barriers
- Younger and older
- Ethnicity/race
- Health status
- Satisfaction

✓ Know the respondents.

Your survey questions should be written so that they encompass your needs for data, but they must also be formulated so that respondents can answer them easily and accurately. Check the appropriateness of the reading level of any questions you write. Reading abilities among respondents may vary considerably, even for the same survey. For example, a survey of parents in a school district may include some people who read extremely well and others who read poorly. You have to decide how to state your questions so that the number of respondents who can read and comprehend all questions is maximized.

Because facing unanswerable questions is extremely frustrating, you need to make sure that your respondents have sufficient knowledge to answer the questions you ask. For example, in a survey to find out about the quality of education, many people may not be able to answer a question like the following:

What role should the Department of Curriculum and Instruction play in setting educational standards for this community?

Unless told, many people might not know about the department's current authority, how it is administered, and how it has been designed to fit into the community. They may not have a clue about the department's role. In their frustration, they may guess, or they may refuse to answer that question or any other question on the survey.

Survey respondents may also have difficulty answering questions that concern their past or future actions and behaviors. For example, if you ask relatively healthy survey respondents about what their health was like exactly 1 year ago, they may be unable to remember, because they have no compelling reason to dwell on their health. Also, if you ask people to tell you who they will elect to the Board of Education in 6 months, they may not yet know. Asking respondents to compare their behavior to that of others also sometimes results in confusion. Asking employees of a particular company to compare the adequacy of child care at that company to the care provided by other firms, for example, is likely to produce poor results unless you are certain that the respondents are familiar with the child care offered at other companies.

✓ **Carefully match what you need to know against the amount of time you have to find out.**

The number of questions you can include in a survey depends largely on the amount of time available for respondents to answer the questions. You can usually include more questions in a half-hour interview than in a 10-minute interview. The number of questions you should include in a survey also depends on what you need to know and how many questions you need to attain adequate measurement.

Suppose that in Survey 1 in Example 1.2, the time allotted for a respondent to fill out the questionnaire is 20 minutes. Suppose also that the survey is supposed to cover 10 topics: educational needs, ethnicity/race, gender, willingness of respondents to participate in job retraining, satisfaction with current educational status, age of parents, how parents manage their household, how parents can care for their children, level of parents' education, and methods for disciplining children for mild, moderate, and severe infractions. The surveyor can ask 1 or more questions to cover each topic or ask 10 questions about any single topic. To decide on which questions to ask, you must balance what you need to know (the specific objectives), the number of questions needed to cover each topic related to each objective, and the amount of time available for the survey.

A good way to get started in determining the number of questions for each topic is to make a chart like the one shown in Example 1.4.

Remember that Survey 1 is to last 20 minutes. To find out if the 35 questions can be answered in the 20 minutes available, the surveyor must try out the questionnaire with potential respondents or people just like them. To determine if the questions cover the topics of the survey adequately, the surveyor can ask experts, search other surveys, and conduct statistical analyses to find out, for example, if parents who are known to cope well answer the questions differently from parents who are known to cope poorly.

✓ Standardize the surveyor.

The ideal standardized surveyor asks all questions the same way every time. When two surveyors who are conducting the same survey are indistinguishable from one another in their delivery and findings, they are standardized.

Standardized surveyors can take human form, as in face-to-face or telephone interviews, or they can take the form of self-administered questionnaires. A self-administered questionnaire can be mailed to respondents or completed in a specially designated area, such as a clinic waiting room, a classroom, or a personnel office. Example 1.5 illustrates the use of standardized surveyors.

EXAMPLE 1.4
Topics, Number of Questions, and Information Collected

Topic	Number of Questions	Information Collected
Educational level	1	Last year of school completed
Educational needs	10	Whether had training for specific jobs (e.g., sales, nurse's aide)
Ethnicity/race	1	African American, White but not Latino, Latino/Latina, Chinese, Southeast Asian, other
Gender	1	Male/Female
Satisfaction with current educational status	1	Yes/No
Willingness to participate in job retraining	1	If needed: yes, no, do not know, or not sure
Age	1	Whether under 18 years of age, between 18 and 20, between 21 and 30, and over 30
Managing a household	6	Manage financial affairs (e.g., balance checkbook, shop for food for a week, monitor household repairs)
Caring for the child	5	Doctor's visits, supervise schoolwork, know names of friends
Discipline methods	8	Method (e.g., talking, hitting, yelling) for mild (e.g., not answering a question), moderate (e.g., coming home more than an hour late), and severe (e.g., not coming home at all) infractions
Total	35	

EXAMPLE 1.5
Standardized Surveyors

1. A survey of parents is conducted to find out if they are willing to participate in a program to prevent child abuse and neglect. A 25-item questionnaire is mailed to 200 parents. The questionnaire was tried out with 50 parents before it was considered suitable. The original version had 35 questions, but the parents who served as test respondents felt that it took too much time to answer. If 10 or more of the test respondents either would not or could not complete particular questions, those questions were omitted. All questions are accompanied by four answer choices, and the respondent is asked to circle the one "best" answer.

2. Interviews were conducted to compare the views of managers and sales staff regarding a program to introduce more flexible hours for employees. The Human Resources Department trained five HR staff members to conduct the interviews. The training took 6 hours, and quality checks of a sample of interviews were made to ensure that each interviewer followed very strict question-asking guidelines.

✓ **Standardize the response format.**

A standardized format asks each respondent to select from a list of preset choices. Example 1.6 distinguishes between standardized formats and other types.

Some people may have difficulty with standardized question-and-response formats. They may object to the structure or be unfamiliar with it. When this happens, the surveyor should try to find another standardized format that is acceptable to the respondents or look for an alternative way of getting the information. One way some surveyors make the structure of a standardized format more palatable for respondents is by offering the questions and choices on videotape.

✓ **Remember that questions are asked in a social, cultural, and economic context.**

In the two survey situations described in Example 1.2, the survey instruments are to be translated from English into other languages. Whenever you must undertake such translation for a survey instrument, you need to ensure that you are asking questions that are meaningful to people speaking the languages you are using. You should rely on survey experts and potential respondents to help with the wording of the questions. Remember also to budget time and money for these activities.

Another contextual factor to consider is whether the answers will be anonymous. If so, you may be posing different kinds of questions than you would otherwise. Surveyors agree generally that respondents are more willing to answer "sensitive" questions about personal behaviors and beliefs when surveys are anonymous (that is, the identities of respondents are not known) than when they are simply promised confidentiality or when respondents' names are common knowledge.

EXAMPLE 1.6
Standardized and Other Response Formats

Standardized Format

Directions: To what extent do you agree with the following statements about the purpose of pretesting self-administered survey questionnaires? In a pretest, a draft of the survey is tried out with a sample of people, and their reviews are incorporated into the final version. *Circle one choice for each statement.*

Purpose of Pretesting	Strongly Agree (1)	Agree (2)	Disagree (3)	Strongly Disagree (4)	No Opinion (5)
To find out if the questions are appropriate for the respondents	1	2	3	4	5
To determine if any questions are misleading	1	2	3	4	5
To examine whether surveyors can appropriately use the survey forms	1	2	3	4	5
To determine if the information obtained by the survey is reliable	1	2	3	4	5
To determine if the information obtained by the survey is valid	1	2	3	4	5

Example 1.6 continued

Unstandardized Format

Directions: Explain the extent of your agreement with the following statement:

"Self-administered questionnaires should be tried out in advance of their use to see if they provide consistent and accurate data. An advance trial means testing the logistics of the survey (the ease with which the interviewers can record responses) as well as the survey form itself."

Write your explanation here:

Guidelines for Asking Survey Questions

You may find that in your own survey, some of these guidelines are more important than others.

ASK PURPOSEFUL QUESTIONS

Purposeful questions are those that are logically related to the survey's objectives. In a survey about airline travel, respondents will expect questions about airlines' food, service, on-time records, and so on. If you need to ask questions that do not seem to be about airline travel (about age or reading habits, for instance), explain your reasons: "Some of our questions are about your background and preferences so that we can examine whether Uniting Airlines is meeting the needs of all its passengers."

ASK CONCRETE QUESTIONS

A concrete question is precise and unambiguous. Questions may be defined as precise and unambiguous when, without prompting, two or more potential respondents agree on the words used in the question. For example, suppose you want to find out about people's perceptions of their health, and you ask them to describe their health. A person who is generally well but has been sick in the past week might answer differently from another individual who was desperately ill all year but is now feeling better. To help make such a question more concrete, add a time period:

Less concrete: How would you describe your health?

More concrete: In the past 3 months, how would you describe your health?

The more detail you can provide in your question, the more reliable the answer is likely to be. For example, instead of asking about usual or typical behavior in a given period, ask about a specific time period, as illustrated in Example 1.7.

EXAMPLE 1.7
Using Specific Time Periods
to Make Questions More Concrete

Poor: How often do you exercise in a typical week?

Better: How often did you exercise during the past week? (Start with today's date and count back 7 days.)

Detailed questions always help to produce reliable answers. For example, if you are surveying responses to a play, rather than just asking a general question about the respondent's enjoyment of the play, decide on the components of the play that are the most important to the survey, as in these examples.

Less concrete: Did you enjoy the play?

More concrete: Did you enjoy the first act of the play?

Even more concrete: Did you find the comedy scenes in the play's first act funny?

EXERCISE

Make these three questions more concrete and describe how you improved specificity.

1. How satisfactory was your stay at the hotel?

2. What is the best way to improve health care?

3. Which restaurants do you eat in most frequently?

• •
POSSIBLE ANSWERS

1. How satisfactory was room service during your stay at the hotel?

   The question has been made more specific in that it now focuses on one aspect of the hotel stay: room service.

2. What is the best way to improve the quality of preventive health care?

   The question is more specific in that it now concentrates on a particular area for improvement: the quality of preventive care.

3. In the past 3 months, which New York restaurants did you eat in most frequently?

   A time period and a place have been set: in the past 3 months and New York.

USE TIME PERIODS THAT ARE RELATED
TO THE IMPORTANCE OF THE QUESTION

Periods of a year or more can be used for major life events like the purchase of a house, occurrence of serious illness, birth of a child, or death of a parent. Periods of a month or less should be used for questions that are less important. Asking people to remember relatively unimportant events over long periods of time leads to too much guessing. You do not want the period to be too short, either, because the event in question may not have occurred during the interval. Example 1.8 illustrates good and poor use of time periods in survey questions.

EXAMPLE 1.8
Use of Time Periods in Survey Questions

Poor: How long did it usually take for you to fall asleep during the past 6 months?

Comment: Too much time has probably elapsed for the respondent to recall accurately. Also, the amount of time to fall asleep may have varied considerably, making estimation a difficult task.

Better: How long did it usually take for you to fall asleep during the past 2 weeks?

Poor: In reference to your car accident of a year ago, how many visits have you made to a physician in the past 6 weeks?

Comment: The number of visits made to the doctor in the past 6 weeks is probably different from the number made in the first weeks after the accident.

Better: In reference to your car accident of a year ago, look at the following list and tell how many visits you have made to a physician.

USE CONVENTIONAL LANGUAGE

A survey is not a conversation. To get accurate information, survey questions rely on standard grammar, punctuation, and spelling. You should use words that maximize understanding for everyone involved in the survey. This is often difficult to do. All questions should be reviewed and tested by people who are proficient in reading and speaking the language in which the survey is written, by content experts, and by potential respondents.

Guidelines for Using Conventional Language When Asking Survey Questions

USE COMPLETE SENTENCES

Complete sentences, whether as statements or questions, express clear and complete thoughts, as illustrated in Example 1.9.

EXAMPLE 1.9
Using Complete Sentences and Questions

Poor: Place of residence?

Comment: Place of residence means different things to different people. For example, I might answer Los Angeles, but another respondent might say California, the United States, or 15 Pine Road.

Better: What is the name of the city where you currently live?

Poor: Accidents among children are . . .

Comment: This statement is unclear. A respondent might say "terrible," "the leading cause of death among children under the age of 12 years," "under-reported," "a public health problem," and so on.

Better: Indicate the extent of your agreement with the statement "Accidents among children are a public health problem in the United States."

AVOID ABBREVIATIONS

Avoid using abbreviations and acronyms in your questions unless you are certain that they are commonly understood. Most people probably are familiar with USA and FBI, and many would be familiar with the abbreviations for their own cities, states, provinces, universities, and so on. But don't count on it. If in doubt, spell it out, as shown in Example 1.10.

EXAMPLE 1.10
Avoiding Abreviations

Poor: In your view, does USC provide a liberal arts education worth the university's yearly tuition?

Comment: If this question is being asked of many Californians, they will understand USC to be the University of Southern California. But for others, USC can mean the University of South Carolina or the University of Southern Connecticut.

Better: In your view, does the University of Southern California provide a liberal arts education worth the university's yearly tuition?

AVOID SLANG AND COLLOQUIAL EXPRESSIONS

Avoid using slang and colloquialisms because they go out of fashion quickly and not everybody keeps up with the newest expressions. There are some exceptions, however. You may want to use slang that is familiar to your respondents in a survey of a homogeneous group who share a special language, such as workers in the same job or profession, people with similar health or social problems, and teenagers.

The problem in using slang and colloquialisms is that if you plan to report the results of the survey to a general audience, you will need to translate the slang, and less-than-expert translation may result in loss of meaning.

BE CAREFUL OF JARGON AND TECHNICAL EXPRESSIONS

It is best to avoid the use of jargon and technical terms in your survey questions unless you have good reason to believe that all of your respondents are familiar with the terms. As with the use of slang, however, you must then be concerned with how understandable a wider audience will find the results.

EXAMPLE 1.11
Avoiding Jargon and Technical Terms

Poor: Should a summative evaluation of Head Start be commissioned by the U.S. government?

Comment: The term *summative evaluation* is used among some specialists in program evaluation. It means a review of the activities and accomplishments of a completed program or of one that has been in existence for a long time.

Better: Should the U.S. government commission a history of Head Start to review that program's activities and accomplishments?

HAVE THE QUESTIONS REVIEWED BY EXPERTS

Experts are individuals who are knowledgeable about survey question writing or the subject matter addressed by a survey. Experts can tell you which survey questions appear too complex to be administered easily and which are too long or too difficult to be answered accurately.

HAVE THE QUESTIONS REVIEWED BY POTENTIAL RESPONDENTS

Potential respondents are people who are eligible to be part of the survey sample—that is, the kind of people you want to hear from. For example, if you plan to survey teens in high school to find out about their eating habits, then your reviewers should be high school teenagers. A review by potential respondents helps to guarantee that the survey's questions are meaningful and inclusive of all important ideas.

ADOPT OR ADAPT QUESTIONS THAT HAVE BEEN USED SUCCESSFULLY IN OTHER SURVEYS

A great many survey questions are available to the public. Among these are questions asked by the U.S. Census. Such questions have already been reviewed, used, and shown to collect accurate information. Use them for your survey, when appropriate.

USE SHORTER QUESTIONS WHEN YOU NEED TO SAVE TIME, MINIMIZE READING, OR ARE SATISFIED WITH BRIEF ANSWERS

Shorter questions save time and require relatively little reading. The answers to such questions also tend to provide less detailed information. Longer questions often provide background information to respondents and help them recall or think about why they did something or hold a particular view.

Short: Have you ever traveled to another country? If yes, how important was the scenery in your decision to take a trip?

Long: Travel to other countries has become increasingly popular among Americans. Have you ever traveled to another country? If yes, you might have traveled to other countries to enjoy their scenery. How important was the scenery in your decision to take a trip?

Long questions are useful for getting information on sensitive concerns (e.g., health and sexual habits) and socially controversial issues (e.g., gun control and substance abuse). When using longer questions in self-administered questionnaires, you need to consider the time they take to read and answer. Example 1.12 shows the use of a longer question.

EXAMPLE 1.12
A Sample Longer Question

"A diagnosis of prostate cancer can have a profound effect on the quality of life of older men and their families. At least three treatments are available to men with prostate cancer: observation, surgery, and radiation. Your husband [partner] has chosen surgery. How much influence did you have in your husband's [partner's] choice of treatment?"

USE LOADED QUESTIONS, IF NECESSARY, BUT BE CAUTIOUS

Surveyors sometimes deliberately load questions to get information on embarrassing or controversial topics. The purpose of loading a question is to encourage the respondent to give a "true" response rather than just one that is socially acceptable. Two kinds of loading are often used, as illustrated in Example 1.13.

EXAMPLE 1.13
Using Loaded Questions to Prompt the Respondent

1. *You are not alone.* Parents get really angry at their children sometimes. In the past week, have you been really angry at your son?

2. *You are in the best company.* Many prominent people have publicly admitted that they have sought help for problems related to alcohol abuse. In the past year, have you been to see a physician or other health professional because you thought you were drinking too much?

Use loaded questions with caution. People may see through them, get annoyed, and either not answer the questions or answer them inaccurately.

AVOID BIASING WORDS AND PHRASES

Biasing words and phrases elicit emotional responses that may have little to do with the issues addressed by the survey. They are considered biasing because they trigger emotional responses or prejudice. Some words and phrases with this quality include *abortion, pro-life, creationism, secular humanism,* and *the right to bear arms.*

The biases people attach to words tend to change with time. The words *socialist* and *communist* now rarely evoke much emotional response in the United States, although they did so for 50 years. Other words and phrases simply die out or are discarded or replaced. *Drug addict,* for example, has generally been replaced by *substance abuser* (or *user*).

Bias may arise in your survey if you do not fully understand the culture and values of the respondents and ask questions that are inadvertently offensive. To guard against this possibility, you need to have all questions reviewed and pilot-tested before you use them.

AVOID TWO-EDGED QUESTIONS

A two-edged question contains two separate ideas. An example is "Do you think we should continue to use tax money to support arts and sports programs in the public schools?" This question is really twofold: "Do you think we should continue to use tax money to support art programs?" and "Do you think we should continue to use tax money to support sports programs?" Certainly, some people would endorse spending tax money to support the arts programs, some to support sports, others both, and still others neither. No matter what the respondent answers to a two-edged question, however, you will not know exactly what he or she means. To avoid asking such questions, check the use of the word *and* in your questions.

AVOID NEGATIVE QUESTIONS

Negative questions are difficult for many respondents to answer because they require an exercise in logical thinking. For example, suppose a question asks respondents if they agree or disagree with the statement "The United Nations should not have more authority to intervene in a nation's military affairs." Some respondents will fail to read the word *not*. Others will mistakenly translate the negative into the positive and believe the question is "Do I think the United Nations should have more authority to intervene in a nation's military affairs?" If you do use a negative question, be sure to emphasize the negative word: "The United Nations should **not** have more authority to intervene in military affairs."

2 Keep Questions Closed or Open Them Up?

Questions take one of two primary forms. When they require respondents to use their own words in answering, they are called *open* or *open-ended*. When the answers are preselected for the respondent to choose from, they are called *closed* or *closed-ended*. In general, closed questions are considered more efficient and reliable than open-ended questions for getting information from groups of people. Both types have advantages and limitations.

Open-Ended Questions

Open-ended questions allow respondents to give answers in their own words. These questions are useful if you are interested in getting unanticipated answers or in learning about the world as your respondents really see it. Also, some respondents prefer to state their views in their own words, and sometimes this results in quotable material that can be

useful for the survey report. The responses to open questions, however, are often difficult to compare and interpret.
Consider the question in Example 2.1.

EXAMPLE 2.1
An Open-Ended Question and Three Answers

Question: How often during the past month did you find
  yourself having difficulty trying to calm down?

Answer 1: Not often

Answer 2: About 10% of the time

Answer 3: Much less often than the month before

The answers respondents give to open-ended questions must
be cataloged and interpreted. For instance, looking at the
answers in Example 2.1, does 10% of the time (Answer 2)
mean not often (Answer 1)? How does Answer 3 compare to
the other two? Open-ended questions are used primarily in
surveys concerned with gathering data about individuals
rather than groups. Experts in qualitative research are experi-
enced in cataloging and interpreting responses to open-
ended questions.

Closed or Closed-Ended Questions

Closed-ended questions provide respondents with preselected answers from which to choose. Such questions are
more difficult to write than open questions because one
needs to know the possible answers, or response choices, in
advance. Some respondents prefer closed-ended questions
because they are either unwilling or unable to express themselves while being surveyed.

Closed-ended questions produce standardized data that can be analyzed statistically, and statistical analysis is essential for making sense of survey data for groups of people (e.g., teams, schools, teens, the elderly, Americans). Also, because what is expected of the respondent is more clearly spelled out in such questions, the answers have a better chance of being reliable or consistent over time. Closed questions are easy to standardize. Example 2.2 shows a closed question.

EXAMPLE 2.2
A Closed Question

How often during the past month did you find yourself having difficulty trying to calm down?

[Circle **one** number]

Always	1
Very often	2
Fairly often	3
Sometimes	4
Almost never	5
Never	6

How do you know when to use open-ended questions and when to use closed questions? The following checklist can help you to decide.

Checklist for Deciding Between
Open- and Closed-Ended Questions

	√ If Yes, Use Open-Ended Questions	√ If Yes, Use Closed-Ended Questions
Purpose	Respondents' own words are essential (to please respondent, to obtain quotes, to obtain testimony)	You want data that are rated or ranked (on a scale of *very poor* to *very good,* for example), and you have a good idea of how to order the ratings in advance
Respondent characteristics	Respondents are capable of providing answers in their own words Respondents are willing to provide answers in their own words	You want respondents to answer using a prespecified set of response choices
Asking the question	You prefer to ask only the open question because the choices are unknown	You prefer that respondents choose among known choices
Analyzing the results	You have the skills to analyze respondents' comments even though answers may vary considerably You can handle responses that appear infrequently	You prefer to count the number of choices
Reporting the results	You will provide individual or grouped verbal responses	You will report statistical data

3 Responses: Choices and Measurement

When a respondent is expected to give an answer in his or her own words, the question is open-ended. When a list of the possible answers to a question is provided for the respondent to choose among, the question is closed. Items on a survey instrument that use open-ended questions consist of the questions alone. Items that use closed-ended questions consist of the question and the response choices.

Response Choices

Response choices, or the choices given to respondents from among which they select their answers, take several forms. **Categorical** or **nominal** (the two terms are often used interchangeably) response choices involve categories, such as male and female. These types of responses have no numerical or preferential values; they are simply correct or incorrect, true or false.

A second type of response choice is called **ordinal**. Respondents who are asked to rate or order the items in a list (say, from very positive to very negative) are given ordinal choices. **Numerical** response choices call for numbers, such as age or height.

Categorical, ordinal, and numerical response choices are illustrated in Example 3.1. The first question in the example asks the respondent to name, or categorize, his or her astrological sign; such a question implicitly gathers information on the month in which each respondent was born. A survey result might be stated as follows: "At least 34% of respondents are Aries, who were born between March 21 and April 19." The second question is different; the information it provides takes the form of a hierarchy. A sample result might be "At least 50% of the sample is under 50 years old, but only 5% of respondents are over 65 years of age." The third question determines age by asking the respondent for a number. A survey result stated from the information gathered from such a question might be "The average age is 26 years."

EXAMPLE 3.1
Three Common Response Choices

1. **Categorical (or nominal):** Name or categorize your astrological sign. Check **one** only.

Aquarius	❏	Leo	❏
Pisces	❏	Virgo	❏
Aries	❏	Libra	❏
Taurus	❏	Scorpio	❏
Gemini	❏	Sagittarius	❏
Cancer	❏	Capricorn	❏

Example 3.1 continued

2. **Ordinal:** Tell into which of the following age groups, given in order from youngest to oldest, you fit best. Circle **yes** or **no** for each.

Years of Age	1. Yes	2. No
Under 25	1	2
25-30	1	2
31-40	1	2
41-55	1	2
56-65	1	2
Over 65	1	2

3. **Numerical:** As of your most recent birthday, what number of years tells how old you are?

_____ years old

Which kinds of response choices should you use? To decide, you must first know what each can do for your survey. Consider the three questions in Example 3.2, which were designed for a survey whose main purpose is to guide curriculum development in colleges. As in Example 3.1, the three types of response choices are represented: categorical, ordinal, and numerical.

Suppose the objectives of the survey in Example 3.2 are these:

- Identify books and plays that are considered important reading for graduates.

- Examine the relationship between the books and plays people read and those they rate as being important.

- Examine the relationship between respondents' ages and the books and plays they rate most and least important.

EXAMPLE 3.2
Three Questions
About Important Literature

1. **Nominal or categorical:** Which of these books or plays have you read? Circle **yes** or **no** for each choice.

Have you read this?	Yes (1)	No (2)
Oedipus Rex	1	2
Pride and Prejudice	1	2
The Vicar of Wakefield	1	2
The Bible	1	2
Moby Dick	1	2
The Glass Menagerie	1	2

2. **Ordinal:** How important to a college graduate's education is each of the following books and plays? Use the following scale to make your ratings:

   1 = Definitely unimportant
   2 = Probably unimportant
   3 = Probably important
   4 = Definitely important
   5 = No opinion/Don't know

Eample 3.2 continued

Books/Plays	Circle ONE for each literary work				
Oedipus Rex	1	2	3	4	5
Pride and Prejudice	1	2	3	4	5
The Vicar of Wakefield	1	2	3	4	5
The Bible	1	2	3	4	5
Moby Dick	1	2	3	4	5
The Glass Menagerie	1	2	3	4	5

3. **Numerical:** What is your date of birth?

_____ _____ 19 _____

Month   Day   Year

- Each of the questions in Example 3.2 produces a particular kind of information. The first question asks respondents to tell if they have read each of six works of literature. The second question asks respondents to use a continuum divided into four points (with a "no opinion/don't know" option) to indicate how important each of the six works is. The third question asks respondents to specify the month, day, and year of their birth.

- Survey questions typically require three basic tasks of respondents, use three "scales," and produce three measurement patterns or types of data. The three questions in Examples 3.1 and 3.2 represent the three kinds of tasks, scales, and data.

- The first question in Example 3.2 asks respondents to tell whether or not they fit into one of two categories: read this book or did not read this book. Data or measures like these have no natural numerical values and are called *categorical* or *nominal*. A hypothetical survey finding that uses categorical data might take this form: "More than 75% of the respondents read at least one book or play on the list, but no one read all six. Of 75 respondents, 46 (61.3%) indicated they had read the Bible, the most frequently read book." Categorical measures result in counts and frequencies expressed as numbers and percentages.

- The second measurement pattern, represented by the second question in Example 3.2, is called *ordinal*. A response is made to fit on a continuum or scale that is ordered from positive (very important) to negative (very unimportant). The information from scales like this is called ordinal because an ordered set of answers results. Ordinal data consist of the numbers and percentages of people who select each point on the scale. In some cases, you may find it expedient to compute the average response: the average rating of importance across all respondents. Sample survey results might take a form like this: "Of 75 respondents completing this question, 43 (57.3%) rated each book or play as definitely or probably important. The average ratings ranged from 3.7 for the Bible to 2.0 for *The Vicar of Wakefield*."

- Surveys often ask respondents for *numerical* data. In Example 3.2, respondents are asked for their birth dates. From these dates, the surveyor can calculate each respondent's age. Age is considered a numerical and continuous measure, starting with zero and ending with the age of the oldest person in the survey. When you have numerical data, you can perform many statistical operations. Typical survey findings might appear as follows: "The average age of the respondents was 43 years. The oldest person was 79 years, and the youngest was 23. We found no relation between age and ratings of importance."

Categorical or Nominal Measures: How to Get Them

The first question in Example 3.2 asks respondents to answer yes or no regarding whether they have read each of the named books and plays. "Yes" and "no" are categories into which the responses must be placed. Other commonly used response categories are "present" or "absent" and "applies" or "does not apply." If you ask 100 respondents to name the countries of their birth, and 20 answer France and 80 say the United States, you have categorical data that can be described this way:

	Yes	No
Born in France?	20	80
Born in the United States?	80	20

When you ask people the names of their countries of birth, their astrological signs, their ethnicities, and so on, you are collecting categorical data. Such data are also called *nominal* because the names determine the categories. See Example 3.3 for some typical kinds of questions that produce nominal or categorical information. Other examples of nominal or categorical measures are questions like these:

- Which of the following medical problems do you have? Hypertension; diabetes; low back pain

- Are you currently married? Living with someone but not married? Not currently married and not living with someone? Married but living alone?

- Do you have a B.A.? M.A.? M.Ed.? M.S.W.? Ph.D.? M.D.?

EXAMPLE 3.3
Nominal or Categorical Data From Surveys

1. Indicate your gender by circling the appropriate number.

	1. Yes	2. No
Female	1	2
Male	1	2

2. Which best describes your race/ethnicity? Circle **one** choice only.

Race/Ethnicity	1. Yes	2. No
White, not Latino	1	2
Latino	1	2
African American	1	2
Native American	1	2
Asian (please specify _____)	1	2

CATEGORICAL RESPONSES AND WHO IS ELIGIBLE

Nominal or categorical responses put respondents into categories, such as male or female, Native American or African American. Questions that ask respondents to categorize or name themselves are used to get demographic information and help decide who should be included in (or excluded from) a survey. Suppose you are planning to ask people to rate the importance of six books and plays. To get accurate information, you want to survey people who know what they are doing. You might decide to exclude potential respondents who have read only four or fewer of the books and plays of interest. A question asking for categorical answers would then be appropriate:

- Which of the following books have you read? Check all that apply.

    _____ *Pride and Prejudice*
    _____ *The Vicar of Wakefield*
    _____ *The Bible*
    _____ *Moby Dick*
    _____ *Madame Bovary*

The responses to "check all that apply" questions are almost always categorical, because each check means "Yes, I belong in the category." Each category or choice that is left blank is assumed to mean "No, I do not belong."

CATEGORICAL RESPONSES ARE EXCLUSIVE

Categorical response choices should be mutually exclusive. Compare the following examples of poor and better questions and response categories.

Poor: Which of the following best describes you?

	1. Yes	2. No
Professional	1	2
Registered nurse	1	2
Nurse practitioner	1	2
Administrator	1	2
Nurse midwife	1	2

Comment: The categories for the responses are not mutually exclusive. The choice "professional" can include all of the remaining categories; that is, a nurse practitioner, a registered nurse, a nurse midwife, and an administrator can all be considered professionals. To confuse matters even more, nurse practitioners, administrators, and nurse midwives may all be registered nurses.

Better: Which of the following best describes you? Answer yes *or* no for each category.

	1. Yes	2. No
Registered nurse, but no bachelor's degree	1	2
Registered nurse with a bachelor's degree	1	2
Registered nurse with a master's degree	1	2

CATEGORICAL RESPONSES ARE INCLUSIVE

Categorical response categories should be inclusive and exhaustive. You should include all categories on which you hope to get information. The following are illustrations of two questions that might be asked in a survey of lawyers to identify how many of them have specific expertise in various kinds of legal problems.

Poor: Which one of the following best describes your primary expertise?

Landlord-tenant problems   ❑
Consumer problems   ❑
Traffic cases   ❑
Other (specify) _____   ❑

Comment: These categories are not exhaustive. The survey is likely to produce more responses in the "other" category than in the three that are listed.

Better: Which one of the following best describes your primary expertise?

Landlord-tenant problems	❏
Consumer problems	❏
Traffic cases	❏
Small claims	❏
Misdemeanors	❏
Felony cases	❏
Wills	❏
Personal injury claims	❏
Domestic relations	❏
Adoption	❏
Tax	❏
Real estate	❏
Bankruptcy	❏
Poverty	❏
Other (specify) _____	❏

CATEGORICAL RESPONSES AND MEANING

A major issue when you ask questions that produce categorical responses is how to group responses so that they are meaningful. A general rule is to use groups that make sense in the survey and that also will be useful when you report the results of the survey. Suppose you are conducting a survey of elderly people and you want to know how many in your survey fall into certain categories or age groups. You could frame your question as in Example 3.4.

The question and responses used in this example are fairly standard. If you look at surveys of older persons, you will find that the response groups used in the question are typical. One good way to be sure you are using meaningful categories is to adapt or adopt those used in other surveys. Already existing and in-use choices tend to make reporting easier because they are familiar.

Existing response choices may not always suffice to meet the needs of a particular survey, however; then, of course,

EXAMPLE 3.4
Question for Older People

Which best describes your age group? Circle **one** choice only.

Age Group	1. Yes	2. No
65-74	1	2
75-84	1	2
85-95	1	2
Over 95	1	2

you must create your own. Question 2 in Example 3.3 shows the standard racial/ethnic terms used to describe categories for a survey concerning prenatal care among low-income women in Northern California. At the time of the survey (1992), these groupings accounted for 98% of women who were likely to be in any survey of prenatal care in that geographic region. The terms that are considered acceptable change over time, however, and so the ones used in a particular survey may seem out of place or dated just a few years later. Be cautious in using questions from other surveys and standard terms for such things as job descriptions, names of countries, and income groups.

Example 3.5 shows two questions about age that might be used in a study about individuals' music-listening habits. The purpose of Question 1 is to produce information that can be used in comparing teens and nonteens. All people 31 or older are grouped together.

EXAMPLE 3.5
Choosing Response Choices

1. We conducted a survey to compare teens and others in their music-listening habits. We asked this question:

Which best describes your age? Circle **one.**

Years of Age	1. Yes	2. No
12 or younger	1	2
13-14	1	2
15-17	1	2
18-21	1	2
22-30	1	2
31 or older	1	2

2. We conducted a survey to compare the music-listening habits of people of differing ages. We asked the following question:

Which best describes your age? Circle **one.**

Years of Age	1. Yes	2. No
20 or younger	1	2
21-30	1	2
31-40	1	2
41-50	1	2
51-60	1	2
61 or older	1	2

The aim of Question 2 is to obtain data for comparing people of differing ages. The groupings are based on the following assumptions:

1. Music-listening habits vary according to age decade (e.g., 31-40 and 51-60).

2. All people under 20 years of age have similar listening habits and all those 61 and older have similar listening habits.

3. The differences in music-listening habits between people under 20 and between those 61 and older are not important for the survey's purposes.

Questions With Ordered Responses: How to Get Ordinal Data Using Common Rating Scales

Questions that ask respondents to order their responses are ordinal measures. Question 2 in Example 3.2 is a typical ordinal measure. In the question, respondents are asked to create an order by rating importance on a scale from 1 to 4. In so doing, they are making an implicit statement about the relative importance of one literary work ("definitely important") over another ("definitely not important"). When responses are ordered or placed in ordered groupings along one dimension, you have ordinal data. The most familiar kinds of ordinal data come from scales such as the following:

- Strongly agree, agree, neither agree nor disagree, disagree, strongly disagree

- Excellent, very good, good, fair, poor

- Always, very often, fairly often, sometimes, almost never, never

- Completely satisfied, very satisfied, somewhat satisfied, somewhat dissatisfied, very dissatisfied, completely dissatisfied

Ordinal measures are extremely common in surveys. In fact, typical surveys tend to have more ordinal measures than any other kind. When you are asking questions that require respondents to order their answers, you need to be concerned with the content of the choices, the number of choices, and whether or not you should include a middle point and a "do not know" response. You also need to be concerned with grammar and how the question looks on a page or sounds when spoken in person or on the telephone. Tune in on a conversation between Surveyor A and Surveyor B about ordered responses:

A: I am conducting a survey of anxiety and depression in the workplace. I'd like to ask, "In the past month, how often has feeling depressed interfered with doing your job?" What response choices can I use so that I can compare the number of people who feel depressed most often with the number of people who feel depressed least often?

B: You need a set of response choices that are ordered on a scale ranging from "often" to "not often."

A: What scales are available?

B: You have several options. You can use a simple 3-point scale with response choices like "often," sometimes," and "never"; a 4-point scale with choices like "nearly all the time," "some of the time," "a little of the time," and "almost none of the time"; or a 6-point scale with options like "all of the time," "most of the time," "a good bit of the time," "some of the time," "little of the time," and "none of the time." You can also create longer scales if you want. I can even think of situations in which discrete numerical categories might be appropriate. These categories could be "100% of the time," "between 50% and 100% of the time," and "less than 50% of the time."

A: How do I make my decision?

B: Before I answer, I want to raise some issues you should consider in asking respondents to order their responses, such as whether to include a middle point ("neither agree nor disagree," for example) and whether to include a "don't know" or "no opinion" choice.

A: Do you know of some guidelines for me to use in asking these types of questions and determining response choices?

B: You're in luck. I just came across a set.

Guidelines for Asking Closed Questions and Determining Ordered Responses or Scales

USE A MEANINGFUL SCALE

A meaningful scale is one that makes sense in terms of the survey's specific objectives. In the preceding conversation, Surveyor A wants to compare people in terms of the frequency of their depression, and Surveyor B suggests a number of kinds of response choices. To choose among them, Surveyor A can do any or all of the following:

- Ask potential respondents which scale is best.

- Ask other surveyors to help select a scale.

- Try one or more scales on a preliminary basis and select the one that gives a good "spread" of answers (you do not want everyone to choose just one point on the scale) and is meaningful to the respondent.

CONSIDER FIVE TYPES OF RESPONSE OPTIONS

Endorsement: Definitely true, true, don't know, false, definitely false

---

Frequency: Always, very often, fairly often, sometimes, almost never, never

Intensity: None, very mild, mild, moderate, severe

Influence: Big problem, moderate problem, small problem, very small problem, no problem

Comparison: Much more than others, somewhat more than others, about the same as others, somewhat less than others, much less than others

EXERCISE

Surveyor A wants to study the frequency with which depression interferes with job performance. Suppose the surveyor asks you for a question that will result in comparative information. Write the question.

• •

ANSWER

Compared to your usual performance on the job, how has your depression affected your performance in the past 4 weeks?

Please circle ONE response

Much worse than usual	1
Somewhat worse than usual	2
About the same as usual	3
Somewhat better than usual	4
Much better than usual	5

BALANCE ALL RESPONSES

A scale is balanced when the two endpoints mean the opposite of each other and the intervals between the points on the scale are about equal. "Much worse" (see the preceding exercise) is the opposite of "much better," and the meaning of the interval between "much worse" and "somewhat worse" is similar in degree to that between "somewhat better" and "much better." "About the same as usual" appears to fit in the middle. Of course, language is imprecise, and the intervals may be less equal than they appear on the face of it. That's why you should try out all questions before you use them. Examples of how to balance scales follow:

Poor:	Poor:
Yes, constantly	Very happy
Yes, very often	Somewhat happy
Yes, once	Neither happy nor unhappy
No, never	Not very happy
Better:	Better:
Yes, constantly	Very happy
Yes, very often	Happy
Yes, fairly often	Somewhat happy
Yes, a couple of times	Neither happy nor unhappy
Yes, once	Somewhat unhappy
No, never	Unhappy
	Very unhappy

USE A NEUTRAL RESPONSE CATEGORY ONLY IF IT IS VALID

Provide a neutral category only when you are sure it is a valid response. A neutral category is either a middle point ("neither happy nor unhappy") or a "no opinion/don't know" option. Some surveyors believe that neutral choices provide respondents with an excuse for not answering questions. If you think your respondents might react this way to neutral choices, pretest your questions with and without the neutral choices and compare the results. How many responses cluster around the middle point? Do some respondents resent not having a middle point? As part of the pretesting process, ask the respondents about the scale. Did they encounter any problems in using it? Would another set of responses be more appropriate?

USE 5- TO 7-POINT RATING SCALES

Current thinking suggests that 5- to 7-point scales are adequate for the majority of surveys that use ordered responses. Self-administered questionnaires and telephone interviews should probably use 4- or 5-point scales. In-person interviews should use visual aids for scales with 5 or more points on them, such as the following sample:

MUCH WORSE THAN USUAL	1
SOMEWHAT WORSE THAN USUAL	2
ABOUT THE SAME AS USUAL	3
SOMEWHAT BETTER THAN USUAL	4
MUCH BETTER THAN USUAL	5

Conclusive evidence for the superiority of either odd- or even-numbered scales is unavailable. You should use whichever best suits your survey's needs.

PUT THE NEGATIVE END OF THE SCALE FIRST

For questions that are potentially embarrassing or that ask about socially undesirable behaviors or attitudes, you should consider putting the negative end of the scale first, as illustrated in Example 3.6.

EXAMPLE 3.6
Putting the Negative End of the Scale First When Questions May Be Embarrassing

How much do these statements apply to you? Circle **one** number for each line.

Embarrassing Statement	Very Much (4)	Much (3)	A Fair Amount (2)	A Little (1)	Not at All (0)
I find that my clothes do not fit.	4	3	2	1	0
I am uncomfortable with the changes in my body.	4	3	2	1	0
I frequently feel anxious.	4	3	2	1	0

In this example, the negative end of the scale means agreeing that the statement applies "very much." If you put the positive end first (that is, the statement applies "not at all"), people may just select that as the least embarrassing option. Deciding which end of the scale to place first is most important in face-to-face interviews and least important in anonymous self-administered and other mail surveys. If the survey deals with a problem the respondent thinks is important, the direction of the scale may not matter at all. If you were asking the questions in Example 3.6 of cancer patients, for instance, you would not have to worry as much about directionality as you would if the questions were meant for teens.

KEEP QUESTIONNAIRES UNCLUTTERED AND EASY TO COMPLETE

Present all questions in an uncluttered, easy-to-complete way in self-administered questionnaires (including mail questionnaires). You can achieve this by following the rules in Example 3.7.

EXAMPLE 3.7
Rules for Presenting Uncluttered Questions

1. Tell the respondent how and where to mark the responses.

Emphasize any special tasks or requirements in the question, as shown below:

Example

Considering your reading habits, **during the past year** how often did you read the following newspapers, journals, and magazines? Circle **one** for each choice.

Periodical	Never (1)	Rarely (2)	Sometimes (3)	Frequently (4)	Always (5)
New York Times	1	2	3	4	5
Wall Street Journal	1	2	3	4	5
Cosmopolitan	1	2	3	4	5
New England Journal of Medicine	1	2	3	4	5
Sports Illustrated	1	2	3	4	5

Example 3.7 continued

2. Avoid questions with skip patterns in self-administered questionnaires.

A skip pattern is an instruction used in a question that you expect does not apply to all participants. If you must use skip patterns, set them off as clearly as possible, as shown below.

Skip Pattern:

14. Have you had **two years or more in your life** when you felt depressed or sad most days, even if you felt OK sometimes?

❑ No   →   **GO TO QUESTION 15**
❑ Yes ____
                 ↓

14A. Have you felt depressed or sad much of the time in the past year?

❑ Yes   ❑ No

3. Organize responses so that they are readable. Consider the following:

Poor: To what extent do you agree or disagree with the following statements?

1. Each day of work feels as if it will never end.

❑ Strongly agree   ❑ Undecided
❑ Agree   ❑ Disagree
❑ Strongly disagree

Example 3.7 continued

> 2. Most of the time I have to force myself
>   to go to work.
>
>   ❑ Strongly agree   ❑ Undecided
>   ❑ Agree   ❑ Disagree
>   ❑ Strongly disagree

Item 1 is poor because it is unclear whether the respondent should mark the line before his or her choice or the
line following it. For example, the line that precedes
"Agree" is also right next to "Undecided." Item 2 is poor
because the choices are not aligned, and the logic of the
scale disappears.

	Strongly Agree (1)	Agree (2)	Undecided (3)	Disagree (4)	Strongly Disagree (5)
Each day of work feels as if it will never end.	1	2	3	4	5
Most of the time I have to force myself to go to work.	1	2	3	4	5

WRITE QUESTIONS SO THAT INTERVIEWERS CAN DISTINGUISH BETWEEN WORDS TO BE READ TO RESPONDENTS AND WORDS THAT ARE INSTRUCTIONS/OPTIONS

See Example 3.8, where the use of capitalized bold-
face letters tells the interviewer to read the respondent
the option "or someone in your family." The question
for respondents is in regular letters, and the instructions
are capitalized. Notice that the interviewer is asked to
present Card A to the respondent. In-person interview-

ers should use cards that show the scales and the scale points' definitions when respondents are asked to select from among five or more choices. Telephone interviewers should read the choices before asking any questions respondents will answer by using a scale and then repeat the choices for each question.

EXAMPLE 3.8
Distinguishing Among Words for Respondents, Instructions, and Options

Which of the following have you (or **SOMEONE IN YOUR FAMILY**) done in the past year with a neighbor? HAND RESPONDENT CARD A. CODE YES OR NO FOR EACH ITEM ANSWERED.

CARD A

	1. Yes	2. No
Stopped and talked when we met	1	2
Had dinner together at their home or ours	1	2
Had dinner together at a restaurant	1	2
Watched their home when on vacation, or they watched ours	1	2

USE RANKINGS ONLY IF RESPONDENTS CAN SEE OR EASILY REMEMBER ALL CHOICES

Rankings or rank-order scales are a type of ordinal measure in which choices are placed in order from the highest to the lowest (or the other way around). The rank of students in a college senior class is important to graduate school admissions committees, for example. The following is typical of questions that ask respondents to rank their preferences:

- Using the following list, select the **three** most important books or plays that U.S. college graduates should have read.

  Oedipus Rex
  Pride and Prejudice
  The Vicar of Wakefield
  The Bible
  Moby Dick
  The Glass Menagerie
  Other (specify) _____

  Put your choices here.
      Top choice:
      Second choice:
      Third choice:

In telephone interviews, rankings should be limited to two or three alternatives at a time. In self-administered surveys and face-to-face interviews in which visual aids can be used, respondents should not be asked to rank more than five alternatives. If you insist on having many alternatives, you should ask respondents to choose the top two or three and the bottom two or three.

Numerical Measures

Numerical measures ask respondents to produce numbers, as illustrated in Example 3.9. The first question in the example asks the respondent to record the number of the listed books and plays he or she has read. The numbers produced by questions like this are called *discrete*. Other examples of questions that produce discrete data are those that ask respondents how many pregnancies they have had, how many accidents they have had, how many employees work for them, and how many patients they see in a day. The second question in Example 3.9 asks for age. Age can start with zero and go up to the end of the human life span. The numbers produced by questions like this are called continuous. Other examples of continuous data are weight, height, years of survival, and scores on a test.

EXAMPLE 3.9
Numerical Measures

1. How many of the following books and plays have you read?

   Oedipus Rex
   Pride and Prejudice
   The Vicar of Wakefield
   The Bible
   Moby Dick
   The Glass Menagerie
   Number of books and plays I have read: _____

2. If you have read the the Bible:

   How old were you when you first read the Bible?

   _____ years old

3. How important to a college graduate's education is each of the following books and plays? **Mark out** the one number that best

Example 3.9 continued

describes your opinion of importance. The meaning of the numbers is as follows:

1 = Very important
8 = Neither important nor unimportant
15 = Very unimportant

Example

Hamlet   1 2 3 4 5 6 7 8 9 10 11 12 13 14 15

This person has assigned the reading of *Hamlet* a rating of 3.

Draw a line through ONE number in each row.

Oedipus Rex	1	2	3	4	5	6	7	8	9	10	11	12	13	14	15
Pride and Prejudice	1	2	3	4	5	6	7	8	9	10	11	12	13	14	15
The Vicar of Wakefield	1	2	3	4	5	6	7	8	9	10	11	12	13	14	15
The Bible	1	2	3	4	5	6	7	8	9	10	11	12	13	14	15
Moby Dick	1	2	3	4	5	6	7	8	9	10	11	12	13	14	15
The Glass Menagerie	1	2	3	4	5	6	7	8	9	10	11	12	13	14	15

Sometimes numerical data are classified as interval or ratio. With interval data, the distances between numbers or points have real meaning. The most commonly used example is the Fahrenheit temperature scale, on which the 10-point difference between 70° and 80° is the same as the 10-point difference between 40° and 50°. Ratio measurements have a true zero, like the Kelvin temperature scale, on which 50 kelvins is half as warm as 100 kelvins. Because the Fahrenheit scale has an arbitrary zero, 40° is not half as hot as 80°. In practice, very few interval scales exist, and statistically, interval and ratio data tend to be treated the same. Using the terms *numerical scales* and *measures* helps to avoid confusion.

The third question in Example 3.9 asks the respondent to choose a number along a continuum for each of the items. A similar way to obtain numerical data is through the use of rating scales that are presented along a printed line. In the following, respondents are asked to place an "X" on the line to describe the extent of their pain:

    0   1   2   3   4   5   6   7   8   9   10
    _____

No Pain   Moderate Pain   Worst
                                                              Possible Pain

Such scales lend themselves to reports like this: "At least 47% of respondents indicated that they had moderate pain (marking 4, 5, or 6 on the scale), whereas 10% had the worst possible pain (marking 10)."

To aid in interpretation of this kind of scale, you need to decide on a length for the line, say, 10 centimeters or 10 inches. Then you can measure where along the line each respondent makes a mark and compute averages and other statistics. If one person places a mark at 1 inch (the low end of the scale), another at 1.3 inches, and a third at 3.3 inches, the average among the three respondents would be 1 + 1.3 + 3.3 = 5.6/3 = 1.866.

4 Knowledge, Attitudes, and Behavior: Additional Tips for Creating Survey Questions

Although it is conventional in some fields, such as health care, to think of measuring knowledge first and then attitudes and behavior, surveys tend to focus on attitudes.

Feelings and Intensity: Getting at the Attitude

An attitude is a general way of thinking, such as being liberal or conservative or being hostile or peaceable. The term *attitude* is often used interchangeably with the terms *opinion, belief, preference, feeling,* and *value.* The following are typical of survey questions about attitudes:

- Do you favor gun control?

- Should the federal government do more to equalize income differences between the rich and the poor?

- How satisfied are you with your job?

- Which of the following are essential goals of a democratic society?

- Which description comes closest to defining the quality of your life?

- How healthy do you feel?

- Which is the best solution to illegal immigration?

- Do you favor an increase in taxes to support educational programs for very poor children?

Attitudes are very complex entities, and they are difficult to define and measure. What are the characteristics that consistently and accurately distinguish liberals from conservatives? Is there a universal definition of *quality of life*? Aspects of these questions are philosophical, but scientific and technical methods are available for producing attitude scales that are valid for specific survey needs. Psychometricians use these methods to examine the statistical properties of questions to find out if they consistently and accurately distinguish people who have particular attitudes from those who do not.

Attitudes are often contrasted with knowledge and behavior. For example, how a person feels about gun control laws, what that person knows about gun control laws, and what he or she personally does about guns may or may not be related logically.

Most survey experts agree that if you are interested in measuring concepts such as political stance, religiosity, and satisfaction (with job or quality of life or health), and you are not in a position to do a scientific experiment to validate the questions, you should use already existing and proven questions. You can find such questions through online searches as well as library searches of books and journals; by contacting college and university departments of medicine, public health, sociology, political science, and psychology; and by asking colleagues and associates to lend you their questions and measures. Books are available that contain attitudinal questions, but no central, updated clearinghouse exists. The fact is that finding attitude questions and scales is hard work. It can be costly in terms of the amount of time you have to spend to identify the right agency with the right questions. In some cases, you may need to pay to use particular questions. If you plan to use questions from existing surveys, you must check on who owns the copyrights to those surveys and find out whether you need the authors' permission to reproduce some or all of the questions.

Once you have identified existing questions that meet the needs of your survey, you must check carefully to make certain that each is suitable for your survey's respondents. Is the language level appropriate? Does it truly ask what you need to know? You should have any borrowed questions reviewed and pretested.

A good way to examine the usefulness of a question is to ask your pretest respondents to tell you in their own words what the question means to them. This is called *cognitive pretesting*. Tune in on the following dialogue between a surveyor and two potential survey respondents:

Surveyor: We are conducting a survey to find out if you are satisfied with your health care. Question 1 asks you to rate the importance of accessible care. The scale you will use has five response choices: "definitely important," "important," "probably important," "probably not important," and "no opinion." Please tell me in your own words what this question means.

Respondent 1: You are asking me to tell you if I think getting an appointment with a doctor when I need one is important to me.

Respondent 2: To me, accessible care means not having to travel long distances and being able to park when you get there.

Surveyor: Based on what you have said, I see that the term *accessibility* is unclear at the present. The survey needs at least three questions to measure accessible care. The first will ask about the ease of getting an appointment, and the second and third will address time to travel and parking, respectively. I also plan to define the response choices clearly. For example, a response of "very important" to a listed consideration would indicate that it is one that you feel must be addressed or you would choose to go elsewhere for care.

It often helps to think of attitude questions as having at least two components: how respondents feel and how strongly they feel (or believe). This is illustrated in Example 4.1.

EXAMPLE 4.1
Feelings and Intensity in Attitude Questions

Edith Wilson, Eleanor Roosevelt, Nancy Reagan, and Hillary Rodham Clinton, each the spouse of a U.S. president, are said to have had considerable influence on U.S. policy. In general, do you approve of the role these spouses have played? Check **one** choice.

❑ Approve (**ask A**)
❑ Do not approve (**ask A**)
❑ Do not care/No opinion (**stop**)

Example 4.1 continued

A: How strongly do you feel about it? Check **one** choice.

❑ Very strongly
❑ Fairly strongly
❑ Not very strongly

Recall and Time: Getting at Behavior

Behavior refers to what respondents actually do. The following are examples of survey questions about respondents' behavior:

- Which of the following magazines and newspapers do you read at least once a month?

- How often do you exercise?

- Did you vote in the last election?

- How frequently do you go to church?

- In the past 3 years, how often did you apply for federal grants?

All questions about behavior are concerned with time, duration, or frequency. Each of the preceding questions specifies a time period: at least once a month, how frequently, the last election, and within the past 3 years.

When developing your survey questions, you should choose time periods that meet the survey's needs and that make sense to the respondent. You can obtain reliable information about events and activities that occurred years ago if they are important. People remember births, deaths, marriages, divorces, buying their first houses, and so on. They also remember what they were doing at the time of great historical events, such as wars and assassinations, and during natural disasters such as fires, floods, and earthquakes. For most other kinds of events, you should not expect people to remember past about a year's time. You can, however, use yearly periods primarily for summary information:

- About how much money did you spend on vacations away from home in the past year?

- In the past 12 months, how often did you go for bicycle rides of 5 or more miles?

Asking respondents to give specific information about their behaviors over long periods of time leads to omissions:

Poor: In the past year, which of the following items of children's clothing did you buy from Outdoors Clothing Company?

Comment: Unless respondents have bought very few clothes for their children or buy exclusively from Outdoors Clothing Company, they might very easily forget.

Better: In the past 3 months, which of the following items of children's clothing did you buy from Outdoors Clothing Company?

Questions concerning very short periods of time can adversely affect the accuracy or validity of answers about behavior:

Poor: In the past week, how often did you buy coffee, tea, bottled water, diet soda, or regular soda?

Comment: A question like this may produce invalid results because respondents may not have purchased any of the items during the past week. Nevertheless, because they do purchase and use such items regularly, they may overreport by indicating a purchase in the past week that really occurred the week before.

Better: In the past 3 weeks, how often did you buy coffee, tea, bottled water, diet soda, or regular soda?

Because questions about behavior have a time element, you are dependent on your respondents' ability to recall. To jog respondents' memories, use lists such as the one shown in Example 4.2. The advantage of using lists is that they can remind respondents of events they may have forgotten. To be maximally helpful, lists should be as inclusive as possible without being too long; lists that go on for many pages can be confusing and boring for respondents. One way to get around this problem is to divide a question into component parts, as illustrated in Example 4.3.

EXAMPLE 4.2
Using a List to Help Respondents Remember Their Actions

This question is about your leisure activities. Since last January, did you do any of these activities? Check **yes** or **no** for each.

	Yes (1)	No (2)
Go to a movie	1	2
Eat out for pleasure	1	2
Window-shop	1	2
Go to the theater	1	2
Read for pleasure	1	2
Go for a run	1	2
Go for a hike	1	2
Ride a bicycle	1	2
Go fishing	1	2
Do gardening	1	2

EXAMPLE 4.3
Dividing the Question:
How to Avoid Long Lists and
Still Get the Information on Behaviors You Need

1. Since last January, have you participated in any of the following activities? Answer **yes** or **no** for each.

Shopping for pleasure	1	2	If **yes**, answer Question 3
Religious groups	1	2	If **yes**, answer Question 5

2. Since last January, did you play any of the following sports? Answer **yes** or **no** for each sport.

	Yes (1)	No (2)
Basketball	1	2
Baseball	1	2
Football	1	2
Bowling	1	2
Other—please name:	1	2
Other—please name:	1	2

Using lists can also have a disadvantage: By presenting lists to respondents, you may encourage them to use only the categories named in the lists, and this may result in a loss of information. To encourage respondents to provide information on all their relevant behaviors, you can add an "other" category to a list, as in Question 2 in Example 4.3. If you add this option, however, you are including an open-ended question, and you must be prepared to interpret and catalog the answers.

EXERCISE

Will the questions in Examples 4.2 and 4.3 produce categorical, ordinal, or numerical data?

• •
ANSWER

Categorical

Regulating Difficulty and Threat: Getting at Knowledge

Knowledge questions are included in surveys to achieve the following objectives:

- Determine if people have enough knowledge about a topic to warrant asking their opinions about it

- Identify gaps in knowledge that warrant education, advertising, publicity, or other kinds of information campaigns

- Help explain attitudes and behavior

Example 4.4 illustrates the three main uses of knowledge questions.

EXAMPLE 4.4
Using Knowledge Questions in Surveys

The University Medical Center is concerned that women are not routinely getting Pap smears. These screening tests are essential for early diagnosis of cervical cancer. A survey is taken of all women who come for gynecological services in a 1-year period.

Knowledge of a Topic. A primary survey purpose is to find out what women know. Accordingly, questions are asked about knowledge of the purpose of Pap smears, how they are performed, and how frequently they should be obtained.

Educational Needs. The answers to the questions are used to find out if an educational campaign is needed and, if so, what topics should be included. The survey's results reveal that nearly 60% of the women do not correctly answer the question about the purpose of the test. Only 20% know how often to have a Pap smear, using guidelines set by the American Cancer Society or the American College of Obstetricians and Gynecologists (the recommendations of the two groups differ). Nearly 92% of women who say they had at least one Pap smear know how it is performed. Based on these findings, the surveyors recommend the preparation of educational brochures in English, Spanish, and Portuguese, the main languages spoken by the medical center's patients. The survey team also recommends a media campaign to encourage women to seek Pap smears.

Example 4.4 continued

Explaining Attitudes and Behavior. One survey question asks about the convenience of clinic hours. The survey team compares the women who say they favor increased clinic hours for screening tests with those who do not. The team's analysis demonstrates that women who correctly answered the questions about the purpose of Pap tests are definitely more favorably disposed (margin of 10 to 1) toward increased hours of clinic operation.

The boundary between attitude and knowledge questions is sometimes blurry. Consider these questions:

1. Using your best guess, what percentage of people do not report some of their pay to the Internal Revenue Service?

2. In your view, what is the best way to prevent influenza in people over 75 years of age?

Are these questions designed to gain information on attitudes or knowledge? The first question looks like a knowledge question because it asks for a fact or a percentage. Estimates do exist of the proportion of people earning money and not declaring it to the IRS, but because most of us probably do not know what that percentage is, we would have to guess. For many of us, our guesses would be as much a reflection of how much cheating we think is going on as an attempt to come up with an accurate estimate. The second question seems like an attitude question, but in fact it is a knowledge question, because a correct answer is available: Give them flu shots.

Knowledge questions are sometimes disguised so as to reduce their threatening appearance. This is done with phrases like "in your opinion," "using your best guess," and "have you heard or have you read that . . . ?" Knowledge questions can vary widely in difficulty. The easiest questions are relatively general and ask for recall of current or significant information. The most difficult questions ask the respondent to recall, understand, interpret, and apply information in innovative ways. Consider this example:

Easier: Have you heard or read about President Kennedy's assassination?

More difficult: From this list, select the name of President Kennedy's probable assassin.

Even more difficult: Five cities are circled on this map. Please point to the circle that indicates the city in which President Kennedy was assassinated.

The first question is the easiest because the significance of the assassination suggests that nearly everyone (not just Americans) will have heard or read about the assassination. The second question requires recall of a name. President Kennedy was assassinated in 1963, and for many, the assassin's name has faded from memory. Others may have never learned the name. The use of a list may help respondents to remember the name if they ever learned it. The third question requires knowledge of the name of the city in which the assassination took place and its location on a map; because it involves recall and understanding of geography, it is the hardest of the three questions.

Most surveys of knowledge are not achievement tests in the classical sense. They are not used to grade or promote students or to find out what they have learned. You may be more interested in finding out how many respondents do *not* know about something. Many surveys of knowledge include "do not know" or "no opinion" response choices. These choices also help remove some of the threat associated with knowledge questions. Suppose you were surveying respondents about the physical environment. You might ask a question like the following:

> A fossil of an ocean fish was found in a rock outcrop on a mountain. Which of the following best describes the meaning of this finding? Select **one** choice only.
>
>> Fish once lived on the mountain.
>> The relative humidity was once very high.
>> The mountain was raised up after the fish died.
>> Fish used to be amphibians like toads and frogs.
>> The fossil fish was probably carried to the mountain
>>   by a great flood.
>> I don't know.

By providing an "I don't know" category, you give people who might otherwise just guess a place to put their responses. But beware—sometimes respondents who are just lazy or who do not want to think about the question will use the "I don't know" option even when they might be able to come up with the correct answer.

Demographics: Who Are the Respondents?

Demographic information consists of facts about a respondent's age, race/ethnicity, education, job, gender, marital status, geographic place of residence, type of residence, size of family, and so on.

Compare the two typical demographic questions about race and ethnicity in Example 4.5. The aim of these two questions is to collect a vital statistic: the race or ethnicity of the respondent. The two questions differ in the following ways:

- Question 1 gives the choice of "Black or Negro," whereas Question 2 gives the choice "Black, African American."

- Question 1 refers to "Indians (Amer.)" and asks for the name of the enrolled or principal tribe, whereas Question 2 gives the choice of "Native American

(American Indian)" and does not ask for the name of the respondent's tribe.

■ Question 1 includes as choices "Hawaiian," "Korean," "Asian Indian," "Guamanian," "Eskimo," and "Aleut," whereas Question 2 does not mention these but does include "Chinese Vietnamese."

EXAMPLE 4.5
Two Questions About Race and Ethnicity

Question 1

4. Race

Fill ONE circle for the race that you consider yourself to be.

        ○ White

        ○ Black or Negro

If **Indian (Amer.)**, print
the name of the
enrolled or principal
tribe. ----------------------→
        ○ Indian (Amer.) (Print the name of the
           enrolled or principal tribe) ↓

        ○ Eskimo

        ○ Aleut

              Asian or Pacific Islander (API)

If **Other Asian or Pacific Islander (API)**, print one group: for example, Hmong, Fijian, Laotian, Thai, Tongan, Pakistani, Cambodian, and so on. ----------------------→

If **Other race**, ----------→
print race

○ Chinese	○ Japanese
○ Filipino	○ Asian Indian
○ Hawaiian	○ Samoan
○ Korean	○ Guamanian
○ Vietnamese	○ Other API ↓

        ○ Other race (Print race) ↑

Example 4.5 continued

Question 2

What is your race/ethnicity? Check **one** only.

❑ White, non-Latino

❑ White, Latino (or Hispanic)

❑ Black, African American

❑ Asian: Chinese, Japanese

❑ Southeast Asian: Vietnamese, Cambodian, Hmong, Laotian, Chinese Vietnamese

❑ Other Asian (not Chinese, Japanese, or Southeast Asian)

❑ Pacific Islander (Samoan, Filipino, etc.)

❑ Native American (American Indian)

❑ Other (specify)

_____

Questions 1 and 2 in Example 4.5 take different forms because they were posed for surveys with distinctly different purposes and groups of respondents. Question 1 comes from the U.S. Bureau of the Census's official 1990 Census form. The question was asked of everyone in the United States in 1989. Question 2 comes from a 1991 survey of low-income women who participated in a federally funded project in California to improve maternal and infant outcomes through prenatal care.

Surveys differ in their purposes and thus in the persons who are targeted as respondents. Before asking for demographic information, you should learn about the likely characteristics of your target group. Question 1 in Example 4.5 was asked in the context of a survey concerning the demographic characteristics of everyone in the United States. Question 2 was asked in a survey designed to gather information only about low-income women in one state. If the Census Bureau had asked its race/ethnicity question in the form of Question 2, many races would have been lumped into "other," and a great deal of work would have been necessary to unscramble categories. If the prenatal study had attempted to gather information on race/ethnicity by asking Question 1, many categories might have remained unchecked, and the study would not have obtained data on the number of respondents who were Chinese Vietnamese, a group that was important in the population of concern in the study.

Another difference between Questions 1 and 2 is found in the use of language. In the 1990 Census, the U.S. Census Bureau used the classification "Negro." By 1991, this term was no longer favored, and the prenatal study team elected to use "African American." At about the same time, "Native American" began to coexist with and even supplant "American Indian" as a category, and Question 2's response choices also reflect this.

Note also that Question 2 offers as one of its choices "White, Latino (or Hispanic)," but Question 1 does not include a comparable choice. People who might be described as "White, Latino" constitute a large segment of the U.S. population, but, at least in 1990, Hispanics (or Latinos/Latinas) were not, strictly speaking, considered a racial or ethnic group by the U.S. Bureau of the Census. The Census Bureau asked about Spanish *origin,* and the prenatal care study asked about country of birth, as shown in Example 4.6.

An important distinction between the two questions is in the specificity of the responses. The Census Bureau's ques-

EXAMPLE 4.6
Asking About Origin or Country of Birth

1. Asked by the Bureau of the Census:

7. Is this person of Spanish/Hispanic origin?

Fill ONE circle for each person.

- O   No (not Spanish/Hispanic)
- O   Yes, Mexican, Mexican-Am., Chicano
- O   Yes, Puerto Rican
- O   Yes, Cuban
- O   Yes, other Spanish/Hispanic (Print one group, for example: Argentinean, Colombian, Dominican, Nicaraguan, Salvadoran, Spaniard, and so on.) ↓

If **Yes, other Spanish/Hispanic,** print one group ----->

| |
----

2. Asked in a survey of low-income women receiving prenatal care in California:

If you are White, Latina (or Hispanic), then what is the country of your birth? Check **one** only.

❑   United States

❑   Mexico

❑   Central America

❑   Caribbean

❑   South America

❑   Spain or Portugal

❑   Other: _____

tion provides data on the precise country of birth in South and Central America. The California question asks for less detailed information about these continents but singles out Mexico because of the large number of people of Mexican origin in California.

Why do surveyors ask respondents demographic questions? A major reason is to tell who the respondents are. How old are they? Where do they live? What is their race/ethnicity? Demographic data are also useful in helping to explain the results of surveys. In a survey of child-rearing practices, you might be seeking information that can help you answer questions like these: Do differences exist between younger and older respondents? Among respondents from differing parts of the country? Among those from differing countries of origin?

Demographic data are also needed to help explore the findings of research and of other surveys. Consider the task of the survey team described in Example 4.7.

EXAMPLE 4.7
Exploring With Demographics

The community is concerned that many people are not taking advantage of preventive health services such as immunizations for children, influenza vaccinations for the elderly, prenatal care, and yearly mammograms for women over 50 years of age. A number of surveys are planned to help explore the barriers that deter people from using these services.

A team has designed the first survey to find out about barriers to the use of prenatal care. Their review of the published research reveals that currently unmarried women begin receiving prenatal care late in their pregnancies and do not receive care consistently. They also have poor birth outcomes. When compared to the

Example 4.7 continued

babies of married women, the babies of unmarried mothers are more frequently of low weight and premature. The survey team is interested in exploring factors other than (or together with) marital status that may help explain inappropriate use of prenatal care.

The survey team reasons that currently unmarried pregnant women may be younger than other pregnant women. Births to very young mothers are riskier than other births, so age may be a contributing factor to the poor outcomes. The team also suggests that unmarried women may be poorer than others, and that being poor is often associated with lack of access to and use of health services. They also consider that education may be a factor in the use of health services. If they find that the women in the community who are currently unmarried and pregnant are also relatively young, then the surveyors will be especially interested in finding out about the extent of their completed education. Accordingly, the survey team includes demographic questions on women's birth dates, income, and education.

Age, Income, and Education

To get precise information about respondents' ages, you need to ask for date of birth. If you ask respondents simply to state their age, some people will tell you their age that day and others will tell you their age on their next birthday, which happens to be next week. In a survey that takes, say, 6 months to complete, even the most accurate statements of age are difficult to interpret. Suppose you ask Respondent A his age today, Respondent B her age 2 weeks from today, and Respondent C his age 6 months from today. When you begin to summarize the data 1 year from today, do you compute the ages on the basis of where the respondents were 12 months ago? Do you make any allowances for the fact that by the time you got around to Respondent C, Respondents A and B had aged? If you have your respondents' dates of birth, you can much more easily compute exact frequencies and averages. You can pick one date—say, 6 months after the start of a 1-year survey—and compute everyone's exact age on that date.

Income questions are often "sensitive." In the United States, a person's income is considered a private, even personal matter, and asking respondents about their income requires special care. One way of protecting respondents' privacy and yet getting the data you need is to ask respondents where their income falls in a listing of categories, such as between $40,000 and $50,000 or between $50,001 and $60,000. Remember to provide mutually exclusive categories:

> *Poor:* Which best describes your personal income in 2002? Check **one** only.
>
> $35,000 or less   ❑
>
> $35,000 to $55,000   ❑
>
> $55,000 to $75,000   ❑
>
> $75,000 or more   ❑

> *Comment:* These categories overlap, so that a person whose income is at the high or low end of a category could correctly choose either one.

> *Better:* Which best describes your personal income in 2002? Check **one** only.
>
> $35,000 or less   ❑
>
> $35,001 to $55,000   ❑
>
> $55,001 to $75,000   ❑
>
> $75,001 or more   ❑

When you are asking income questions with categorical choices, make sure the categories are meaningful. If your respondents are wealthier people, you should give them many choices above the median income for the community, whereas if your respondents are poorer, you should give them many choices below the median, as illustrated in Example 4.8.

Whenever possible, you should ask for precise information about income. The U.S. Census Bureau's income questions are very specific: Respondents are asked about their total income and are also asked to specify income from wages, salaries, commissions, and tips; self-employment income from farms and other businesses; income from interest and dividends; rental income; income from estates and trusts; income from royalties; income from social security or railroad retirement pay; Supplemental Security Income, Aid to Families with Dependent Children, or other public assis-

EXAMPLE 4.8
Asking Questions
About Income in Two Settings

Setting 1

A survey is being conducted of all people who used Travelmore Travel Agency for three or more trips out of the country that lasted at least 2 weeks. One question asks about household income:

Which of the following best describes *your* income this current year? Check **one** only.

❑ $50,000 or less

❑ $50,001 to $100,000

❑ $100,001 to $200,000

❑ $200,001 or more

Example 4.8 continued

Setting 2

A survey is being conducted to find out where low-income families obtain mental health services. People are approached outside schools, churches, and super-markets. One question asks about income:

Which of the following best describes *your* income this current year? Check **one** only.

❑ $10,000 or less

❑ $10,001 to $20,000

❑ $20,001 to $30,000

❑ $30,001 or more

tance or welfare; income from retirement, survivor, or disability pensions; and income from child support payments, unemployment benefits, and alimony.

When asking questions about income, you must specify a time period. Do you want to know about average income over 3 years? Total income over the past year? You must also decide if you want a particular person's income or the household's. If you want the household income, you must define *household* as it pertains to income. An infant may be in the household but is not likely to be contributing income to it. Two or more unrelated adults may constitute a household if they contribute to some predefined proportion of the household's income.

You should select questions about education that are suitable to the needs of your survey. In a survey of physicians, questions regarding education will have different response choices from those given to a broader group of respondents, as illustrated in Example 4.9. In a survey of teens' education, you would want to specify most categories before 12th grade

EXAMPLE 4.9
Two Questions About Education

Question 1

A survey of physicians in an academic medical center is interested in finding out how many of them have obtained academic degrees. The survey asks this question:

Do you have any of the following degrees? Circle **yes** or **no** for each degree listed.

	Yes (1)	No (2)
Master's degree in public health	1	2
Master's degree in business administration	1	2
Ph.D. (specify field: _____)	1	2
Doctor of Dental Surgery	1	2
Juris Doctor	1	2
Doctor of Veterinary Medicine	1	2
Other (specify: _____)	1	2
Other (specify: _____)	1	2

Question 2

A survey of customers at Travelmore Travel Agency asks this question about their education:

How much school have you completed? Check **one** for the highest level completed or degree received. If currently enrolled in school, check the level of previous grade attended or highest degree received.

- ❏ 12th grade or less
- ❏ High school graduate or equivalent
- ❏ Some college but no degree
- ❏ Associate degree (academic or occupational)
- ❏ Bachelor's degree
- ❏ Master's degree
- ❏ Professional school degree (such as M.D., L.L.B., J.D., D.D.S., D.V.M.)
- ❏ Doctorate (such as Ph.D., Ed.D., Dr.P.H.)

(such as 9th grade, 8th grade, 7th grade, 6th grade, or lower); you may also wish to include "Other" as a category. The following guidelines will help you to formulate the kinds of questions you need to get demographic information.

Guidelines for Asking Questions on Vital Statistics and Demographics

Learn the characteristics of the survey's targeted respondents, so that the response categories make sense. You can find out about your intended respondents by checking census data, interviewing some individuals from the targeted group, asking others who know about the respondent group, and reviewing recent literature.

Decide on an appropriate level of specificity. An appropriate level is one that will meet the needs of the survey but not be too cumbersome for the respondent. Remember, questions in a self-administered survey or a telephone interview should have no more than four or five response categories. An in-person interviewer should provide respondents with visual aids if questions have more than five response categories.

Ask for exact information in an open-ended format. One way to avoid having many response categories is to ask respondents to tell you in their own words the answers to demographic questions. Respondents can give their dates of birth, income, ZIP codes, area codes, and so on.

Use current words and terms. The words that are considered appropriate for use in describing people and their backgrounds change over time, and respondents will sometimes find outmoded words to be offensive. The world's geography changes, and people's affiliations and commitments alter. If you borrow questions from other sources, check to be sure that they use words that are contemporary and appropriate. Definitions of terms such as *household* and understandings of concepts such as "wealth" and "poverty" also change over time.

Decide if you want comparability. If you want to compare one group of respondents with another, consider borrowing questions and response choices from other surveys. For example, if you want to compare the education of people in your survey with the education of typical Americans in 2000, then use the education question that was asked in the 2000 U.S. Census. If you borrow questions, check to be sure that the words and terms used are still relevant and that the response choices are meaningful.

5 Special Survey Questions: Factorial, Conjoint, and Online

Factorial Survey Questions: Constant or Changeable Beliefs?

Surveyors use **factorial questions** when they want to find out if people's beliefs are constant or changeable. Take the case of lying. Do you believe that lying is always wrong, or does it depend on the situation? Although most of us believe that lying is wrong, many people will tell lies under certain circumstances. Many believe that telling "white lies" is not wrong; for example, we might tell a little girl she looks beautiful in her new dress even if we think she looks silly, or we will tell a friend we had a great time at his party even if we were bored stiff. Most people do not support lying in more serious situations. For example, most would say that it is wrong to lie in a court of law because telling the truth in that setting is essential if we are to have a just society.

In factorial survey questions, respondents are given one or more vignettes that describe hypothetical situations (little girl in new dress, attendance at a friend's party, testifying in court) and are asked to judge them. To use such questions in your survey, you need to create vignettes that involve factors that vary (variables) and that you know are likely to be associated with the outcome that interests you. Looking at the vignettes in Example 5.1, you can see that the surveyor has determined that eight variables are likely to influence teachers' definitions and reporting (the outcomes): gender of the parent, gender of the child, age of the child, parent's ethnicity, parent's employment status, severity of punishment, type of punishment, and child's behavior.

EXAMPLE 5.1
Factorial Survey Question in Use

Teachers in this state are required to report suspected cases of child abuse and neglect. Do the teachers define child abuse uniformly? How often would they report abuse if they saw it? To find out the answers to these questions, the surveyor creates vignettes to use in a survey of teachers. Each vignette describes a situation that some people may consider to be an instance of child abuse. Certain factors within the vignettes vary (such as the parent's gender, the child's age, and the parent's ethnicity). Two sample vignettes follow.

Vignettes	Is this child abuse?		If you saw this, would you report it?	
The [mother] hits her [12-year-old] [daughter] using [a wooden stick]. The mother is [White] and [unemployed]. The child [appears sullen].	Yes	No	Yes	No
The [father] is rarely at home, and [ignores] his [8-year-old] [son] when he is. The father is [African American] and [employed]. The child [is performing well below average in school].	Yes	No	Yes	No

Example 5.2 shows the several levels the surveyor has identified for each of the variables that appear in brackets in Example 5.1. Several thousand vignettes would be needed to cover all the possible combinations of variables and levels; in the real world, you can probably get respondents to concentrate on 10 to 30 vignettes. The actual number you can use will depend on the complexity of the vignettes and the motivation of the respondents to complete the questions. If there are too many questions, people may get bored or confused. Also, because factorial questions usually require respondents to read more than do other survey questions, you have to be careful that the reading level of your vignettes is appropriate for your respondents. Finally, if the vignettes deal with situations your respondents are unfamiliar with, or that do not interest them, the respondents may give up after completing only two or three questions.

To create vignettes for factorial questions, you should begin by randomly combining the different elements of interest at their various levels. You must ensure that all variables have the same probability of being included in the sur-

EXAMPLE 5.2
Variables and Levels

Variables	Levels
Gender of parent	Male, female
Gender of child	Male, female
Age of child	5-14
Ethnicity of parent	Non-Hispanic White, Hispanic White, African American, South Asian, East Asian, Chinese, Japanese
Employment status	Yes, no
Severity of punishment	Spanking with the hand, hitting with a wooden stick, banging against the wall while shaking, hitting in the face with fist
Type of abuse	Physical, emotional, sexual
Child's behavior	Appearance (e.g., sullen) versus reality (e.g., performs poorly in school)

vey, and that the resulting vignettes make sense. The survey questionnaire itself will consist of a random selection of vignettes from the entire pool of vignettes; each respondent should receive a different combination of vignettes. If you have 400 persons who complete 25 vignettes each, you will have 400 × 25 or 10,000 responses.

The advantage of factorial surveys is that they allow you to maximize the internal validity associated with experimental designs and the external validity features of a statistical survey (one in which the analytic units—the vignettes—have been randomly sampled). The following guidelines will help you in for creating factorial survey questions.

Guidelines for Creating Factorial Survey Questions

- *Identify specific survey objectives.* Before you begin to design the survey and its questions, you must be able to describe each of the survey's objectives with a simple phrase beginning with a verb in infinitive form (e.g., "to identify," "to understand," "to examine"). In Example 5.2, the objectives are as follows:

  – To identify the variables that teachers say they associate with child abuse

  – To identify the variables that are associated with teachers' stated willingness to report child abuse

- *Justify your choices of the variables that form the framework for the vignettes.* Knowledge of the variables and their associated levels usually comes from discussions with potential respondents and experts. You can also gain such knowledge by reviewing the literature and asking the advice of practitioners and policy makers. The surveyor who created the list of

---

variables and their associated levels shown in Example 5.2 derived those variables and levels from personal experience gained in caring for abused children and from the literature on child abuse and neglect. For instance, the literature shows that the gender of the perpetrator influences people's opinions on the nature of adult behavior toward children. The surveyor therefore included the gender of the parent as a variable.

- *Assign the variables randomly to the vignettes.* Random assignment helps guarantee that every variable has an equal chance of inclusion in a vignette. You should verify that the vignettes make sense by trying them out. In surveys with many variables, you may come up with vignettes that are implausible and should be omitted.

- *Ensure that the vignettes are readable.* Factorial surveys require respondents to do more reading than do other surveys. Try out the vignettes with sample respondents to make certain that they can read and interpret each one. Keep the vignettes short, and limit the number you use with respondents who read poorly.

Conjoint Analysis Questions: Which Do You Prefer?

Conjoint analysis is a method of data collection and analysis that is designed to draw out respondents' preferences for goods and services. It was developed by mathematical psychologists and has been used primarily in market research, economics, and health care research. The questions used in conjoint surveys are analogous to those used in factorial surveys. Respondents are given hypothetical vignettes describing products or services and are asked to pick the ones they prefer.

Conjoint analysis is based on the premise that any good or service can be described by its characteristics or attributes and that the extent to which an individual values a good or service depends on how much he or she values the levels of the attributes. Suppose you are working for the marketing manager of a company that manufactures jeans, and she wants to find out how to update the look of the company's product. To do this, the manager wants to find out what kinds of jeans her customers prefer, and she calls on you for advice. You have identified three attributes that influence jeans consumers: color, price, and fabric. Each of these attributes in turn has three levels: Possible colors are blue, black, and white; possible prices are $30, $40, and $50; and possible fabrics are denim, cotton twill, and a blend of cotton and linen.

There are two major approaches to designing questions for a conjoint analysis: the pairwise method and the full-profile method. In the *pairwise method,* also called the *two-factor evaluation,* respondents evaluate two attributes at a time (i.e., conjointly) until all the possible pairs of attributes have been evaluated, as illustrated in Example 5.3. You do not have to ask respondents to consider all possible pairs in a conjoint analysis. As with factorial questions, respondents may become weary or confused if you ask them question after question about pair after pair of attributes. You can use standard experimental designs, such as random selection, to reduce the number of pairwise items you give to each respondent.

In addition to the pairwise approach, conjoint analysis can use the *full-profile method,* also called *multiple-factor evaluation.* In this approach, full or complete profiles of the good or service are constructed for all the attributes (see Example 5.4). In a full profile, the respondent is presented with one complete description of the product. The description takes into account all attributes of interest, so if there are many attributes, the description can be quite long. In order to

EXAMPLE 5.3
Partial Basis for Pairwise Questions in a Conjoint Survey

		Color		
		Blue	Black	White
Fabric	Denim			
	Cotton			
	Blend			

Sample question: Which color do you prefer: blue denim or black denim?

		Color		
		Blue	Black	White
Price	$30			
	$40			
	$50			

Sample question: How much would you be willing to pay for white jeans: $30 or $40?

		Fabric		
		Denim	Cotton	Blend
Price	$30			
	$40			
	$50			

Sample question: How much would you be willing to pay for denim jeans: $30 or $40?

reduce respondent burden, you can use special methods (e.g., a special class of fractional designs called orthogonal arrays) to diminish the number of full-profile scenarios that each respondent is required to address.

EXAMPLE 5.4
Conjoint Analysis Question
Using a Full-Profile Approach:
Choosing One of Two Profiles

Color	White
Fabric	Blend
Price	$40

Versus

Color	Blue
Fabric	Blend
Price	$60

Which approach is better? Should you use pairwise or full-profile items? The pairwise approach is easier for respondents because they only have to consider two attributes at a time. But the pairwise approach requires more evaluations than the full-profile approach. Also, the task may seem unrealistic to the respondent, because people rarely make two judgments at a time when considering the attributes they want in a product.

The evidence suggests that the two approaches produce comparable information. In making your choice between approaches, you should consider the purpose of the conjoint analysis and your respondents' reading level and motivation.

Once you choose an approach, you can ask respondents to rank or rate the scenarios. In Example 5.5, a respondent who has been asked to rank nine possible choices of fabric and color has marked white linen as the top choice and black cotton as the second choice. The respondent's least-favored choice for jeans is a blue blend.

EXAMPLE 5.5
Ranking Color and Fabric in a Pairwise Question

Directions: Please rank each color and fabric combination on a scale of 1 to 9. A rank of 1 is your top choice. A rank of 9 is your bottom choice.

	White	Black	Blue
Cotton	7	2	4
Linen	1	6	3
Blend	8	5	9

Respondents can also be asked to rate a good's or service's attributes, as in Example 5.6. Consumers tend to prefer rating items to ranking attributes, and in recent years, the use of ratings in surveys has become more common. Another useful type of rating is one in which respondents are given two scenarios and are asked which one of the two they prefer (e.g., "Do you prefer A or B?"). A variation on this "A or B" rating scheme involves the use of a scale, as shown in Example 5.7.

EXAMPLE 5.6
Rating Jeans Profiles

Please rate each of the following using this scale:

5 = Definitely prefer
4 = Probably prefer
3 = No preference
2 = Probably do not prefer
1 = Definitely do not prefer

White linen at $40	5	4	3	2	1
Black linen at $30	5	4	3	2	1
Blue linen at $20	5	4	3	2	1
Blue cotton at $20	5	4	3	2	1
Black blend at $20	5	4	3	2	1
Etc.	5	4	3	2	1

The questions used in conjoint analysis are usually administered in face-to-face interviews. The data analysis relies on a mathematical model to express the fundamental relationships among the attributes and the importance or "utility" assigned to the attributes by respondents.

Conjoint analysis is often done using special computer programs that offer help in the development of questions and allow users to illustrate key attributes to make them more vivid. Most programs include data editors, so that users can create databases for subsequent exportation into spreadsheet or statistical packages. Most of the available software for use with conjoint studies is proprietary, so if you decide to use such software, you must include the costs involved in your survey budget.

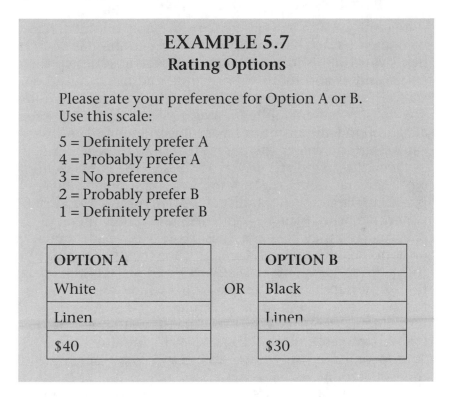

Online Survey Questions

Survey instruments that respondents complete on the Internet look and often act like other self-administered questionnaires. The rules for writing questions for online surveys are almost exactly the same as those that apply to other self-administered questionnaires, whether for paper-and-pencil or computer-based surveys. They include making sure that you have a specific purpose for each question you ask, that you understand the needs of the survey's users, and that you have the resources available to conduct and complete all survey activities. Also, as when you conduct any type of survey, you must respect the cultural and sociopolitical beliefs of respondents and their ability to read and answer each question.

Online surveys are different from paper-and-pencil and computer-assisted surveys in that they can provide respondents with sophisticated audio and visual aids to help them better understand terms they cannot read or do not understand. However, although technology exists that will allow you to supplement online surveys with audio and visual aids, respondents may not have the equipment (e.g., sound cards) that will enable them to hear or view these features.

Even if respondents do have access to the latest technology, they may not know how to use it appropriately, if at all. If you are planning to conduct an online survey, you must be concerned with your respondents' "computer literacy." In particular, do they have the skills to use a keyboard, a mouse, or both in order to scroll through the screens that make up the questionnaire, enter the answers, and perform the operations necessary to go from question to question and submit the completed questionnaire? Some online surveys require respondents to open e-mail attachments or to input particular Web site addresses (URLs) to get to the questionnaires. Some people may use computers but still have difficulty with these operations.

The levels of computer literacy among potential respondents vary greatly. Some people can use practically any type of software, whereas others are mainly familiar with sending e-mail and shopping on the Internet. Generally, individuals respond to online surveys on desktop or laptop computers or on handheld devices. Voice recognition and touch-screen technologies are not yet the norm for these surveys.

On the whole, the types of questions that are appropriate for online surveys are fairly similar to those used in other self-administered questionnaires. In fact, an important and currently unanswered question about online surveys is whether they are simply a technological advance in self-administered survey design or if they are actually a different type of survey altogether.

One major and important difference between the questions you can use in online surveys and those in other types of surveys is that online, even in small surveys (say, those on your company's Intranet), you can easily use color and simple graphics to make your survey more attractive. The comparative effectiveness of color versus the usual black-and-white survey questionnaire is currently unknown, however. Remember that if you plan to use graphics in your online survey, you need to make sure that your intended respondents can easily download any necessary files. Do they have compatible software? Do they have enough disk space to store any files you send them?

DROPDOWN LISTS

Although online surveys rely on the same principles of question writing as do mail surveys and other self-administered surveys, the question and response formats you can use online are more varied. For instance, questions in online surveys can offer responses in **dropdown lists**, as shown in Example 5.8. The respondent clicks on the down arrow following a question, and a list of response choices appears. The respondent then clicks on his or her choice, which immediately appears in the blank bar.

If you use dropdown lists, you must be sure that your respondents know how to use a mouse. Such lists are useful when you want respondents to provide you with information in certain words (e.g., "program," not "intervention"; "interview," not "survey") or when you want information in a specified format (e.g., California, not CA or Cal). Dropdown lists need to offer a finite number of choices (such as the 50 states in the United States, the 6 states of Australia plus the Northern Territories, the 7 days in a week, or the 12 months in a year).

EXAMPLE 5.8
Dropdown Lists

Which of the following most closely matches your current job title?

Product Manager

SELECT ONE

In another form of online question, the respondent selects one of multiple answers. The response choices may be ordinal (as in Example 5.9), nominal (Example 5.10), or numerical (Example 5.11). An "other, please specify" choice may also be offered.

EXAMPLE 5.9
Ordinal Response Choices

Select One Answer from a List of Choices

When are you planning to conduct your next web

survey? (Ordinal Response Choices)

    O Within the next 30 days

    O Within the next 3 months

    O About 6 months from now

    O About a year from now

    O I am not currently planning to conduct

       a web survey

EXAMPLE 5.10
Nominal Response Choices

Which ONE of the following tasks do you perform most frequently in a single day? (Nominal Response Choices)

○ Prepare data output for the program director, statistician and the evaluation team

○ Design data collection procedures, forms and instructions

○ Guide staff through a computer-based survey

○ Process institutional review board requirements

○ Communicate with all regional staff

○ Other, please specify:_____

EXAMPLE 5.11
Numerical Response Choices

In such "select one" questions, when the respondent clicks in the open circle or box (sometimes called a click box, check box, or radio button) next to his or her choice, a check mark or dot appears in the circle or box. The respondent can change an answer by clicking a second time in the same circle or box, making the dot or check mark disappear, and then mark the preferred or correct choice. Alternatively, the respondent can correct an incorrect first choice by clicking a second time in the spot next to his or her preferred choice, and the check mark or dot will disappear from the first choice and move to the second. To avoid confusion, you should provide respondents with instructions on how to answer the questions and how to change their answers if they need to (see Example 5.12).

EXAMPLE 5.12
Instructions for Correcting
an Answer to an Online Survey Question

To answer a question, use the mouse to click on your answer. If you change your mind, you can change your answer by clicking the mouse pointer on a different answer.

CHECK ALL THAT APPLY

Online surveys sometimes include questions with a "check all that apply" option for responses (see Example 5.13). Such questions can be followed by dropdown lists or by lists using radio buttons.

Yes or No to Each Choice: A Variation

Another way to ask a "check all that apply" question is to require the respondent to answer yes or no to each choice (see Example 5.14). From the respondent's point of view, checking all the answers that apply may be easier than answering yes or no to many questions on a list. From the programmer's point of view, however, "check all that apply" questions consist of lists of separate questions for which the answers are yes or no, or present or absent, and must be coded as such. The question in Example 5.13, for instance, is really asking for a yes or no answer to each of several questions: Do you eat pizza? Do you eat pasta? Do you eat bananas? If a respondent clicks on the buttons next to "pizza" and "bananas" but not on the one next to "pasta," you have two yeses and one no. If you assign a code of 1 for yes and a code of 2 for no, the data enterer will enter two 2s and one 1.

EXAMPLE 5.13
A "Check All That Apply" Question

Which of the following foods do you eat at least once a

week? Mark all that apply.

O   Apples

O   Pizza

O   Pasta

O   Bananas

O   Other, please specify:_____

EXAMPLE 5.14
A Variation on "Check All That Apply"

Which of the following foods do you eat at least once a week?

	Yes	No
Apples	○	○
Pizza	○	○
Pasta	○	○
Bananas	○	○
Other, please	○	○
specify_____		

One of the advantages of offering yes/no choices is that if respondents neglect to answer any questions, the online survey software can prompt them to go back and give answers, and prevent them from moving on in the survey until they do. This feature, which protects against missing data, is often cited as one of the main advantages that online surveys have over other surveys. **Online surveys** that require respondents to complete one item before they can move on to the next are called **interactive**.

Some surveyors object to the idea of forcing respondents to provide an answer to one question before they can go on to the next. They point out that no other type of survey forces answers from respondents. They also say that sometimes respondents have legitimate reasons for objecting to particular questions, and that respondents may actually be unable to provide the answers to some questions. The frustration associated with a requirement to answer all questions may lead some respondents to stop before they complete the survey, resulting in missing data.

Some surveyors argue that it may be unethical to force participants to answer questions. One possible way to eliminate this objection may be to provide a "prefer not to answer" or "don't know" choice for every question when all questions must be answered.

SEVERAL QUESTIONS WITH THE SAME RESPONSE CHOICES

One common format used in online surveys to get answers from several questions with the same response choices takes the form shown in Example 5.15. Questions and response choices like these are often used in surveys, and respondents are familiar with them. Respondent familiarity with response scales and how to use them increases reliability.

If you plan to use questions like these in online surveys, you should keep each question and its response choices to a length that fits on one screen, so that the respondent does not have to scroll up to read the choices. If you cannot shorten the question, divide it into two questions. If you are the first person to divide a particular question into two (that is, if you have adapted or adopted the longer form of the question from another survey), you will need to ensure that you have not altered its reliability. You can test this in your pretest and pilot test. In large surveys, you can design an experiment to answer the question: Do I collect the same (equivalent) information when the question is asked in two parts as I do when it is in one part?

EXAMPLE 5.15
Several Questions With
the Same Response Choices

	As Much as I Would Like	Almost as Much as I Would Like	Less than I Would Like	Much Less than I Would Like
I have people who care what happens to me	○	○	○	○
I get love and affection	○	○	○	○
I get chances to talk to someone about problems at work	○	○	○	○
I get chances to talk to someone about my personal problems	○	○	○	○
I get chances to talk about money matters	○	○	○	○

OPEN-ENDED QUESTIONS

Most surveyors prefer to minimize the use of open-ended questions in online surveys, which are designed to permit instant data analysis, and so to yield results quickly. However, in keeping with survey tradition, many surveyors leave space in their online surveys for respondent comments. Example 5.16 shows an open-ended question that is typical of the kind often found in Internet surveys.

User-friendly software programs are available to guide you in choosing and formatting questions for an online survey and arranging them into a questionnaire. To comparison shop, enter the keywords *survey software* into practically any Internet search engine.

EXAMPLE 5.16

6 Survey Question Techniques for the Survey Team: The Focus Group

Surveyors usually spend their time developing, adapting, or adopting questions to ask other people about their knowledge, attitudes, values, and behavior. To make sure that the questions are appropriate and pertinent, surveyors go to others for help. One method they often use to get this help is the group interview called a **focus group.**

A focus group consists of a carefully selected group of people who are brought together to give their opinions and offer their perspectives on specific topics. The participants are chosen because they share many of the characteristics of the people who are the target respondents of the survey, such as age, gender, buying habits, musical interests, literary interests, or health condition.

There are no limits to the topics that focus groups may cover or the characteristics of the people in such groups. Topics may be drawn from business, medicine, the military, education, or any other area of interest. The people in a focus group may be schoolchildren, farmers, consumers, or entrepreneurs, or they may have any other kind of characteristic in common. Surveyors typically use focus groups to help develop the content and format of surveys. However, if you have the resources, you can use focus groups to check on the appropriateness of the language and content of a survey that you have already developed (see Example 6.1).

EXAMPLE 6.1
Checking Language and Content With a Focus Group

The local school district plans to design an educational program to teach young parents about the proper use of car seat belts for their very young children. They have asked you to survey the parents before and after their participation in the program. Many of the parents do not speak or write English very well. You decide to convene a focus group to get advice on how to design the survey. To recruit participants, you hand out flyers in local supermarkets. Two elementary schools also agree to mail invitations to parents of students who are in kindergarten through second grade. After 2 weeks of recruitment, you have found 50 parents who say they are interested. You plan on holding three focus groups with no more than 8 people in each. The criteria you use for selecting each of the 24 parents who will participate from the 50 volunteers include the following:

- Willing to meet at a local church for 2 hours starting at 6:00 P.M. on a weekday

- Has more than one child in kindergarten, first grade, or second grade

- Is a native speaker of Spanish or Korean (the languages in which the focus groups will be held)

The purpose of focus groups is not to educate people. For example, you would not use the focus group described in Example 6.1 to teach the participating parents about the use of seat belts. Nor is the purpose of focus groups to come to consensus about an issue, such as the appropriate use of seat belts. Compare the scenarios in Example 6.2: Scenario 1 describes an appropriate use of a focus group, whereas Scenarios 2 and 3 do not. You should use focus groups when you are looking for a range of ideas and perspectives and you want ideas to emerge from the group. If your aim is to establish group consensus or to educate, focus groups are not the appropriate technique to use.

EXAMPLE 6.2
Use of Focus Groups

Scenario 1: Focus Group

Ten high school students are asked to participate in a focus group to discuss the topic of school violence. What are its causes? What can the school do to prevent violence among students? In the past 6 weeks, there have been four fights at the school, and one student was hurt seriously enough to warrant immediate medical attention.

Scenario 2: Consensus Development

Seven men attend a meeting to formulate guidelines on how to be an effective father. These men were chosen because they have children of their own, and they also work with children as teachers, volunteers, and the like. At the end of their 2-hour meeting, they have come up with 10 specific guidelines.

Example 6.2 continued

Scenario 3: Education

Twelve women attend a structured meeting to discuss methods of self-defense. They see a video and do role-playing. At the end of the meeting, they are given a copy of the video for future viewing.

Focus Group Questions

Focus groups are most often conducted as in-person group discussions. They typically consist of 5 to 10 people who are asked between 5 and 15 questions, and they usually last about 2 hours. How many people participate and the number of questions they are asked are decided on a case-by-case basis. The more people and the more questions you have, the more expensive the process becomes. Focus group participants are usually compensated for their time. A 2-hour focus group will cost from $25 to $200 per participant, depending on where you live and who participates. Also, unless you have experience in leading focused discussions, you will need to hire a skilled moderator; such an expert may charge thousands of dollars.

With conference call technology, it is possible to conduct focus groups over the telephone. This approach enables you to include people throughout the world. One limitation of this method, however, is that it does not allow you to see the participants' reactions to the discussion. If such observation is not important, doing a focus group on the phone can be a very efficient way of enlisting greater representation than just relying on local participants. If you do a telephone focus group, you should keep it to an hour in length. It can help to save time if you send the participants the questions you plan to ask in advance, so they can be prepared for the discussion.

EXAMPLE 6.3
Sample Focus Group Questions

Introduction:
Overall Purpose of Study and Learning Names

Hello. My name is Ana, and we have asked you here to discuss the TechHelp program. TechHelp is designed to provide students with assistance with their hardware and software. Before we begin our discussion, I would like to learn your FIRST names. Let's go around the table and state our names and how long you have been using TechHelp.

[Elicits first names only from each person seated around the table]

More Introductions

We are doing this study for the Department of Information Services, which wants to make sure the customer is satisfied! We will be audiotaping the discussion. Later we will compare our notes to the tapes for accuracy. We will not play any part of the tape for anyone without your permission. Any questions?
Let's begin.

The Questions

Beginning Question

1. How did you learn about TechHelp?

Transition Question

1. Think back. What were your first impressions of the service?

Example 6.3 continued

Key Questions

1. What was most helpful about TechHelp?

2. Did you encounter any problems? If so, what were they?

3. Do you think your class work is affected by access to TechHelp?

4. If you did not have access to TechHelp, where would you go?

Ending Questions

1. Pretend that I am the director of TechHelp. What advice would you give me?

2. We would like assistance in improving TechHelp. Is there anything we didn't cover in today's discussion? Is there anything you would like to add to the discussion?

In all types of focus groups, you should ask carefully prepared open-ended questions in a particular planned sequence that will yield the most complete information. Look at the sequence of the set of questions in Example 6.3, which is fairly standard in focus groups. It is likely that 2 hours will be just sufficient to get complete answers to the eight questions shown in this example.

Checklist for Conducting a Focus Group

✓ Ask questions in a conversational manner.

✓ Keep questions short.

✓ Avoid abbreviations.

✓ Avoid jargon.

✓ Don't let one person dominate the discussion.

✓ Make sure every person participates.

✓ Keep your opinions to yourself.

✓ Check all equipment ahead of time (including audio- and videotapes).

✓ Have someone other than the moderator transcribe the tapes after completion of the focus group.

Checklist for a Good Focus Group Question Sequence

✓ Start with easy questions.

✓ Move from general to specific.

✓ Follow a standard sequence from introduction to ending questions.

Exercises

EXERCISE 1

Read the description of the survey plan and then follow the directions given below it.

Description of Survey Plan

The Outdoors Mail Order Company is planning a mail survey of 150 customers who purchased goods within the past 6 months. A Spanish-language version of the survey will be available upon request. The purpose of the survey is to find out to what extent a market exists for household and kitchen goods with an "outdoors" flavor. For example, many of the fabrics used by the company on furniture and for tablecloths and other linens have patterns of lakes, forests, and mountains. Pots and pans are fashioned after those used on camping trips.

The survey is expected to take no more than 10 minutes and will use only closed-ended questions. All responses will be confidential.

The survey has been designed to answer these questions:

1. How old is the average customer?

2. What proportions of customers live in the different geographic regions of the United States?

3. How many people are willing to purchase each of a selected list of household and kitchen goods sold by the company?

4. On average, how many purchases did customers make in the past 6 months?

5. How satisfied were customers with the service? With the quality of the products?

6. Are differences found in numbers and types of purchases that can be accounted for by age and satisfaction?

The following is an outline of the survey.

Outline for Survey of Market for Household and Kitchen Goods

Topic	Number of Questions	Information Collected
Age	1	Date of birth
Region of the country	1	Northeast, Middle Atlantic, Southeast, Midwest, Northwest, Southwest, West
Kitchen goods	5	Type of kitchen goods would purchase, if any (e.g., furniture, dishes, linens)
Household goods	1	Type of household goods would purchase, if any (e.g., furniture, pictures)
Frequency of past purchases from Outdoors	1	If ever, once before, twice, three or more times
Satisfaction	2	Satisfied with service, with purchase: *extremely satisfied* to *extremely dissatisfied*

Directions

Answer these questions using the description of the survey and the outline.

1. Describe the context in which the survey will take place by describing its purpose, respondents, surveyors, responses, timing, resources, and privacy requirements.

2. Write the questions for the survey using the above outline as your guide. (Do not worry about introducing the survey, the order the questions should take, or any special graphic requirements.)

3. For each question in the survey, tell whether you will be obtaining categorical, ordinal, or numerical data.

EXERCISE 2

Write a survey that answers these questions:

1. Does this book achieve each of its stated objectives?

2. On the whole, how helpful were the book's examples in assisting readers to learn?

3. How practical are each of this book's guidelines and checklists?

4. Do readers usually enjoy reading the text and doing the exercises?

5. Do readers who do and do not recommend this book to others have similar school- or job-related responsibilities?

6. Does a difference exist between younger and older readers in terms of their perceptions of the book's helpfulness and practicality?

EXERCISE 3

Comment on these remarks made by the leader of a focus group session.

Hello. My name is George. We are here today to discuss teenagers and smoking. As you know, smoking among teens is a major problem. About 10% of teens in this school say they smoke at least one cigarette daily, and about 25% smoke at least one once a week. Boys smoke more often than girls. This is a problem because of the health implications of smoking. Today, we are going to discuss methods the school might use to get the no-smoking message across. Let's start by telling us your name. When you give your last name, please spell and pronounce it. . . .

Thanks. Now, you have been selected to participate in this discussion because all of you smoke at least some of the time. I'd like your advice on what would make you stop. Suppose we cut down on your allowance? Would that make you stop? How about if we grounded you for a day? How would you react to that? . . .

I would like to conclude by asking your advice. Suppose you had 3 minutes to advise the principal. What would you say to her? . . .

Have we left out anything? Would you like to say anything before we conclude? It is very important that we come to consensus on this important issue.

ANSWERS

EXERCISE 1

1. The Survey's Context

Purpose. The purpose of the survey is to find out if a market exists for kitchen and household goods that are sold by Outdoors and, if so, to characterize it. The characteristics of concern are age, region of the country, willingness to purchase selected kitchen and household goods, frequency of purchases, and satisfaction with purchases and service.

Respondents. The respondents are 150 customers who ordered from the company within the past 6 months.

Surveyor. The mail survey.

Responses. A variety of responses can be expected, including ratings of satisfaction and categories to describe where people live geographically.

Timing. The survey is to take 10 minutes of each respondent's time.

Resources. A Spanish translation is needed.

Privacy. The responses are to be confidential.

2. Questions for the Survey

What is your date of birth?

_____	___	19___
Month	Day	Year

In which region of the country do you live? Check **one** answer only.

Northeast   ❑
Middle Atlantic   ❑
Southeast   ❑
Midwest   ❑
Northwest   ❑
Southwest   ❑
West   ❑

Check **yes** or **no** to indicate whether you would purchase each of the following if it had an outdoors theme. By outdoors theme, we mean fabrics that depict lakes, rivers, mountains, and so on, and styles that are based on camping, fishing, and hiking gear.

Would you buy each of these kitchen goods if they were similar in appearance to those used when camping, fishing, or hiking and/or if they had an outdoors theme or design?

	Yes (1)	No (2)	Don't Know/ No Opinion (3)
Pots and pans	1	2	3
Flatware (knives, forks, spoons)	1	2	3
Dishes and glasses	1	2	3
Table linens (napkins, placemats, tablecloths)	1	2	3
Floor coverings	1	2	3

Would you buy each of these household goods if they were similar in appearance to those used when camping, fishing, or hiking and/or had an outdoors theme or design?

	Yes (1)	No (2)	Don't Know/ No Opinion (3)
Furniture for the living room	1	2	3
Floor coverings	1	2	3
Pictures and photographs	1	2	3
Bedroom furniture	1	2	3
Furniture for a study or den	1	2	3

In the past 6 months, how many items did you purchase from Outdoors? Select **one** best answer.

1	❏
2 to 4	❏
5 to 10	❏
More than 10	❏

How satisfied are you with Outdoors's service and quality? Circle **one**.

	Extremely Satisfied (4)	Satisfied (3)	Dissatisfied (2)	Extremely Dissatisfied (1)	No Opinion (0)
Service	4	3	2	1	0
Quality	4	3	2	1	0

3. Types of Data Obtained From Each Question

Date of birth:	numerical
Region of the country:	categorical
Willingness to purchase kitchen goods:	categorical
Willingness to purchase household goods:	categorical
Frequency of purchases:	numerical
Satisfaction with service and quality:	ordinal

EXERCISE 2

1. Does this book achieve each of the following objectives? Answer **yes** or **no** for each objective.

Objectives for the Reader	Yes (1)	No (2)	Uncertain/ Don't Know (0)
Understand a survey's context (e.g., cultural, economic, political)	1	2	0
Ask valid survey questions	1	2	0
Compare the characteristics of open and closed questions	1	2	0
Distinguish among response formats that use categorical, ordinal, and numerical measurement	1	2	0
Identify questions that are written correctly	1	2	0
Apply techniques for asking questions to learn about behavior	1	2	0
Apply techniques for asking questions to learn about attitudes	1	2	0
Apply techniques for asking questions to learn about knowledge	1	2	0
Apply techniques for asking questions to learn about demographics	1	2	0

2. On the whole, did the book's examples assist you in learning?

  Please circle **one**.

Definitely yes	1
Probably yes	2
Probably no	3
Definitely no	4
Uncertain/no opinion	5

3. How practical are each of the following guidelines and checklists for asking survey questions? Please rate the practicality of **each** guideline and checklist using this scale:

  1 = Very impractical
  2 = Impractical
  3 = Practical
  4 = Very practical
  0 = Uncertain/no opinion

Please make **one** rating for each of the listed guidelines and checklists.

Guidelines					
Guidelines for Asking Survey Questions	1	2	3	4	0
Guidelines for Using Conventional Language When Asking Survey Questions	1	2	3	4	0
Guidelines for Asking Closed Questions and Determining Ordered Responses or Scales	1	2	3	4	0
Guidelines for Asking Questions on Vital Statistics and Demographics	1	2	3	4	0
Checklists					
Checklist for Deciding the Survey's Context	1	2	3	4	0
Checklist for Deciding Between Open- and Closed-Ended Questions	1	2	3	4	0

Did you usually enjoy reading the text and doing the exercises? Please rate **each**.

	Almost Never (1)	Rarely (2)	Sometimes (3)	Frequently (4)	Almost Always (5)
Reading the text	1	2	3	4	5
Doing the exercises	1	2	3	4	5

2. Do you recommend this book to others who have similar responsibilities for asking survey questions?

   Please circle **one**.

Definitely yes	1
Probably yes	2
Definitely no	3
Probably no	4
Uncertain/no opinion	0

3. For which purposes do you plan to write survey questions? Check all that apply.

Evaluation/research	❑
Policy	❑
Program planning or development	❑
Needs assessment/marketing	❑
Other: _____	❑

4. In which settings do you plan to or are you actually asking survey questions? Check all that apply.

School, college, or university	❑
Government	❑
Business	❑
Health professions	❑
Law	❑
Other: _____	❑

5. What is your date of birth? Write 01 for January, 02 for February, and so on. Write 01 for the first day of the month, 02 for the second, and so on. Write in the last two digits of your year of birth so that 71 would mean 1971 and 82 would mean 1982.

   _____ ____ 19___
   Month Day   Year

EXERCISE 3

Focus groups are designed to get answers to carefully selected questions from people who share certain characteristics and interests. Focus groups are not designed to educate people about a topic or to foster consensus. The leader of the focus group in Exercise 3 spends too much time educating the participants about the problem of smoking. He or she also aims to have the group come to consensus on the questions raised during the discussion. This is an inappropriate outcome for a focus group.

Suggested Readings

Babbie, E. (1990). *Survey research methods.* Belmont, CA: Wadsworth.

Fundamental reference on how to conduct survey research. Includes good examples of survey questions with accompanying rules for asking questions.

Bradburn, N. M., & Sudman, S. (1992). The current status of questionnaire design. In P. N. Biemer, R. M. Groves, L. E. Lyberg, N. A. Mathiowetz, & S. Sudman (Eds.), *Measurement errors in surveys* (pp. 29-40). New York: John Wiley.

Addresses many of the major issues regarding questionnaire design and how to ask questions.

Converse, J. M. (1987). *Survey research in the United States.* Berkeley: University of California Press.

An overview and good examples of how surveys are used in the United States; helpful for understanding the context of survey research.

Couper, M. P., Traugott, M. W., & Lamias, M. J. (2001). Web survey design. *Public Opinion Quarterly, 65,* 231-253.

Many examples of questions used in an Internet study to examine the effects of question format and design on data quality.

Fink, A. (1993). *Evaluation fundamentals: Guiding health programs, research, and policy.* Newbury Park, CA: Sage.

Gives rules for asking questions and responses, provides a checklist for creating or adapting measures, and discusses the roles of categorical, ordinal, and numerical data in measurement and data analysis.

Fink, A., & Kosecoff, J. (1998). *How to conduct surveys: A step-by-step guide* (2nd ed.). Thousand Oaks, CA: Sage.

Gives many examples of survey questions and contains rules and guidelines for asking questions.

Frey, J. H. (1989). *Survey research by telephone* (2nd ed.). Newbury Park, CA: Sage.

Gives excellent examples of questions and how to get needed information through telephone surveys.

Lavrakas, P. J. (1993). *Telephone survey methods: Sampling, selection, and supervision* (2nd ed.). Newbury Park, CA: Sage.

Discusses questions in the context of telephone surveys.

McDowell, I., & Newell, C. (1996). *Measuring health: A guide to rating scales and questionnaires* (2nd ed.). New York: Oxford University Press.

Contains a very good compendium of scales to use in asking questions pertaining to health.

Miller, D. C. (1991). *Handbook of research design and social measurement.* Newbury Park, CA: Sage.

Discusses and defines all possible components of social research. Includes selected sociometric scales and indexes and is a very good source of questions pertaining to social status, group structure, organizational structure, job satisfaction, community, family and marriage, and attitudes.

O'Toole, R., Webster, S. W., O'Toole, A. W., & Lucal, B. (1999). Teachers' recognition and reporting of child abuse: A factorial survey. *Child Abuse & Neglect, 23,* 1083-1101.

An excellent example of factorial questions in use.

Ryan, M. (1999). Using conjoint analysis to take account of patient preferences and go beyond health outcomes: An application to in vitro fertilization. *Social Science & Medicine, 8,* 535-546.

Explains and describes the basic principles of conjoint analysis and provides examples of questions. Discusses the mathematics of conjoint analysis well, and the examples of conjoint analysis in use are well worth reviewing.

Schuman, H., & Presser, S. (1981). *Questions and answers in attitude surveys.* New York: Academic Press.

Raises and addresses many important issues regarding how to design questions about attitudes; includes good examples.

Stewart, A. L., & Ware, J. E. (1992). *Measuring functioning and well-being: The medical outcomes study approach.* Durham, NC: Duke University Press.

Tells of the design and validation of a wide range of self-reported functioning and well-being measures developed for a large U.S. study of health care; very good source of questions.

Sudman, S., & Bradburn, N. M. (1982). *Asking questions.* San Francisco: Jossey-Bass.

Very good source for examples of how to write questions pertaining to attitudes, knowledge, behavior, and demographics.

Glossary

Categorical (or nominal) response choices—Response choices that are divided into categories such as overweight and underweight, satisfactory and unsatisfactory. Such choices have no numerical or preferential values; they are correct or incorrect, true or false.

Closed question (or closed-ended question)—A question for which the respondent is provided preselected answers to choose among (see **open-ended question**).

Conjoint analysis—A method of data collection and analysis that is designed to draw out preferences for goods and services. Respondents are given hypothetical vignettes describing a product or service and are asked to pick the one they prefer.

Dropdown list—A list of response choices offered to respondents in online surveys; a respondent clicks on a down arrow on-screen, and the list of choices appears.

Factorial question—A type of question used to find out how people's beliefs vary from situation to situation. For instance, almost everyone believes that lying is wrong, but many people will tell "white lies" in particular circumstances if they think that telling the truth may cause pain.

Focus group—A carefully selected group of people who are brought together to give their opinions and offer their perspectives on specific topics.

Interactive online survey—A survey conducted online in which the respondent can move to the next question only after he or she has answered the previous one.

Numerical response choices—Response choices involving numbers; used for questions such as age (e.g., number of years) or height (e.g., number of meters).

Open-ended question (or open question)—A question that requires the respondent to use his or her own words in answering (see **closed question**).

Ordinal response choices—Response choices that respondents use to rate or order items, say, from very positive to very negative.

Response choices—The choices from which respondents select their answers (e.g., five choices on a scale of 1 = *strongly agree* to 5 = *strongly disagree*).

Survey—A system for collecting information from or about people in order to describe, compare, or explain their knowledge, attitudes, and behavior.

About the Author

Arlene Fink, Ph.D., is Professor of Medicine and Public Health at the University of California, Los Angeles. She is on the Policy Advisory Board of UCLA's Robert Wood Johnson Clinical Scholars Program, a consultant to the UCLA-Neuropsychiatric Institute Health Services Research Center, and President of Arlene Fink Associates, a research and evaluation company. She has conducted surveys and evaluations throughout the United States and abroad and has trained thousands of health professionals, social scientists, and educators in survey research, program evaluation, and outcomes and effectiveness research. Her published works include more than 100 articles, books, and monographs. She is co-author of *How to Conduct Surveys: A Step-by-Step Guide* and author of *Evaluation Fundamentals: Guiding Health Programs, Research, and Policy; Evaluation for Education and Psychology;* and *Conducting Research Literative Reviews: From Paper to the Internet.*